MOTIVATION AND TEACHING:

A PRACTICAL GUIDE

MOTIVATION AND TEACHING:

A PRACTICAL GUIDE

by
Raymond J. Wlodkowski

National Education Association
Washington, D.C.

Copyright © 1978
National Education Association of the United States

Library of Congress Cataloging in Publication Data

Wlodkowski, Raymond J.
  Motivation and teaching.

  Bibliography: p.
  Includes index.
  1. Motivation in education. 2. Teaching.
3. Learning, Psychology of. I. Title.
LB1065.W59   370.15'4   77-28104

*To my parents, who
introduced me to the
wonder of learning.
R.J.W.*

Preface

I've written a book that I have needed and wanted—but could not find—ever since I started teaching 15 years ago. What I sought then—and what I've tried to create now—is a straightforward, useful, and realistic book about motivation and teaching.

The writing of this book, as well as my experience with students and research, has left me uneasy, yet hopeful, about motivation. As a concept, it is far too complex and continues to defy exact definition and understanding. However, as a category, motivation provides many ideas and approaches that can enhance teaching and increase the opportunity for successful learning. And perhaps, for me, this has been the greatest insight—*that teaching is not and may never be a sure thing, that what makes students learn cannot be guaranteed or totally predicted*. Because although learning is a natural capacity in human beings, it is also an open-ended, creative, and phenomenological process which is unique and constantly changing.

That is why teaching will continue to be a science within an art. For no matter how many fixed rules, precise definitions, and logical strategies we establish, our students by their own individuality and growth will probably continue to defy them.

This book is a guide to assist that art. It strongly encourages planning and using specific motivation factors and strategies with respect to time and place. But this is more technique than art. What you choose and how you create what you've planned will be your art.

Raymond J. Wlodkowski
University of Wisconsin, Milwaukee

Contents

Chapter 1

Motivation: Why Human Behavior Occurs

Historically, for those of us who teach, the quest for motivated students has been analogous to the pursuit of beauty and truth by humankind—the goal is worth pursuing but we have only a slim chance of attaining it in our lifetime. Every teacher wants a motivated class. We know the benefits of having students who are excited by learning. Their vitality and enthusiasm increase our own and provide the fuel for the fire of our involvement and pleasure in the teaching role. With motivated students, communication flows, discipline problems lessen, anxiety decreases, and teaching can be the art that so many of us have been told that it is. With unmotivated students, communication is difficult at best, discipline problems increase, anxiety is heightened, and teaching becomes a badgering, nagging chore. If anything could have ever been made real by wishing for it or wanting it, teachers would have made motivated students the norm long ago.

Why is it so difficult? Why do teachers have to struggle to have motivated students? My answer to this question is a metaphor: Facilitating motivation in students is like taking a car trip from New York to California; you can have all the money necessary, buy a new car, make plans well in advance, organize the needed supplies, make the proper reservations, and have everyone, including yourself, ready to go, but if you lose the ignition key (or get a flat tire, or take a wrong turn, or run out of gas, or lose your money, etc.), you can't go anywhere. The point is that with student motivation, when only one thing goes wrong, the entire process may come to a complete stop. The best lesson plans, the greatest materials, a highly motivated teacher, or the newest curriculum cannot guarantee that students will want to learn continuously.

Others may have more profound answers to the above questions. They may give reasons such as future shock, cultural pluralism, technocracy, deterioration of public education, existential crises, and even the biggest villain of all—television. But my honest feeling is that even in the most perfect of societies, the motivation to learn on a daily basis would be problematical. Almost anything on a daily basis is; working, child rearing, living together, communicating, and even sleeping suffer a similar fate. This is not to say that nothing can be done. Student motivation can be greatly improved—and the rest of this book is committed to that purpose. However, I want to emphasize that while there is a great deal of knowledge that is helpful, there are no miracle methods or universal answers to difficult motivational problems.

What Is Motivation?

If I were to anthropomorphize motivation, I would see it as an obstinate ambiguous creature that stubbornly resists precise definition. Simplistically, motivation deals with why human behavior occurs. Most psychologists and educators use motivation as a word to describe those processes that can (a) arouse and instigate behavior; (b) give direction and purpose to behavior; (c) continue to allow behavior to persist; and (d) lead to choosing or preferring a particular behavior. So whenever we as teachers ask questions such as, "How do I help my students to get started?" or, "What can I do to keep them going?" or, "What should they do next?" we are dealing with issues of motivation.

A sequential pattern of motivation in learning often takes the following form:

Energy→Volition→Direction→Involvement→Completion

Thus, a student who has the capacity to act (*energy*) makes a choice (*volition*) which includes a certain purpose (*direction*) which, when continued (*involvement*), leads to finishing the learning task (*completion*). In this manner a student opens her/his book, decides to do 10 math problems in order to practice division skills, and works through the 10 problems until finished. At any point, that student's teacher might have a problem helping this student to—

1. Open the book.

2. Select 10 problems for practice.

3. Continue to work on the selected problems.

4. Finish all 10 problems.

In this example, there are at least four points in the learning task at which some motivational problem might arise. Multiply this by a normal class size of 25 students who might be engaging in this experience, and we have 100 points of potential motivational friction. (Note that we have said nothing about doing the problems correctly.) If this same teacher has planned five similar learning tasks during a single day, she/he is confronting possibly 500 points of potential motivational friction. This simplistic example undercovers the awesome challenge of effective teaching. It also demonstrates the dynamic continuous process that student motivation involves. Between what gets a student to start and what helps that person to finish a learning task can be an incredible maze of motivational issues.

The Mythology of Motivation and Learning

Another aspect of motivation which makes it a concept that is difficult to understand as well as to apply is that it has a rich, but misleading mythology. There are probably more than five myths that are related to motivation, but I have chosen to illustrate those that seem to have the most negative consequences for both teachers and students.

Myth 1: *When students will not involve themselves in activities or do assigned tasks, they are unmotivated.* One of the most common concerns of teachers is that their students are not motivated. A universal declarative sentence heard in teacher meetings, lounges, etc., is, "(Name) is just not motivated!" to which the heads of our colleagues either nod in agreement or shake in mutual despair. The fact is that if students are behaving, they are usually motivated. They may not be motivated to learn, but they are motivated to do *something*. That something might include day dreaming, talking with a friend, teasing a neighbor, looking for attention, or even fighting, but it would be incorrect to say that they are *not motivated*. In such instances, it is more accurate to say, "(Name) is not motivated to learn with me." The latter statement seems to imply that the motivational problem may have something to do with student volition or proper direction of energy or continued involvement. The former statement implies a lifeless blob and increases a sense of teacher helplessness. Restless behavior is an excellent example of typical student behavior that is often labeled unmotivated. In many such instances, students have the energy (maybe even a little too much energy), but they don't have the direction they want. If we were to go into any high school at 3:00 P.M. on a Friday afternoon, we would find many restless students as well as a few teachers similarly disposed. They all have the energy, but the direction has shifted to what's going to happen after school. And after school dismisses, their motivated behavior is visibly obvious in the enthusiasm with which they leave.

Myth 2: *Teachers motivate students*. Teachers do not motivate students. In fact, no one motivates anyone. We can make things attractive and stimulating. We can provide opportunities and incentives. We can allow for the development of competence and match student interest with learning activities, but we cannot directly motivate students. Just as we are responsible for our own feelings, we are responsible for our own motivation. Between what we do as teachers and what students do as learners are the students' perceptions, values, personalities, and judgments. These elements decide the final outcome of student motivation. There is no direct line of control like a radio switch between teacher behavior and student motivation. Students can be influenced and affected by teachers, but they cannot be directly motivated.

And that is the way it should be, because if it were not so, students would have no responsibility for their learning. They would merely be puppets dependent on the teacher who pulls the strings. They could not take pride in the choices and perseverance that lead to their accomplishments. It is not through obedience but through responsibility that real self-affirmation takes place. In many ways, because we as teachers continue to support the idea that we can motivate students, we allow them and their parents to unquestionably blame us for poor learning. This continues the image of the teacher as the ultimate "learning giver" and prevents the mutual respect and interdependence that are necessary between an effective teacher and a responsible student.

Myth 3: *Since students have to learn in order to survive, making them learn is more important than having them motivated to learn.* There is no doubt that many students can be forced to learn or at least coerced into doing learning tasks. By punishing them, threatening them, and holding back desired activities and objects, we can scare and intimidate students into performing learning-directed behavior. We often do this under the rationale that, "learning to read and write is more important than waiting for students to want to learn." But is it?

Frequently it appears that the more years a student spends in school, the more likely it is that she/he will be turned off to school. American high schools abound with potential dropouts, apathetic students, and discipline problems. We have many "deficit learners"— students who know how to read and write well, but who don't want to pick up a book or compose an essay. Studies demonstrate that financial and public support for schools is declining in many instances because of today's parents' personal negative experiences while gaining their education in American schools.[1]

Finally, there are very few students of normal intelligence who *want* to learn but can't—while there are many who *don't* want to learn but can. My personal opinion about the latter type of students is that they are simply "turned off" to learning. They have learned not to want to learn. Because their learning has been associated with threat, coercion, and fear, the classroom and its associated tasks have become a general aversive stimulus. This aversion produces physical withdrawal in the form of dropping out, skipping classes, and being constantly tardy. Psychological withdrawal occurs in the form of student negativism and apathy. "Making" a student learn appears to have severe long-range effects.

Myth 4: *Threat can facilitate motivation to learn.* Most teachers do not want to employ threat initially as a means of working with students. In fact, we usually rely on threat as a last resort. When our alternative teaching methods and forms of persuasion are ineffective, we become desperate and fall back on ways of treating students that were used on us in our school days. We tell the students that if they don't "shape up," we will call their parents, lower their grades, make them do more work, keep them after school, and on it goes. And, for some students, it seems to work—so we are partially reinforced in our efforts and encouraged to use them again.

What happens to the student who is threatened is the same thing that would happen to us in similar circumstances. She/he feels frightened and resentful of the threatening persons. She/he can get rid of the fear by doing the work, but the resentment usually lingers. Even if the student is not frightened, there is usually resentment because to experience threat is often demeaning to the human personality. For the student, the statement behind this feeling is usually some version of, "They [teachers] shouldn't treat me this way." With resentment come the emotional partners of mistrust and vindictiveness. This results in many forms of passive–aggressive behavior including slower learning, sloppy work, and negativism which lead to more teacher nagging and frustration. The teacher is now prone to threaten more easily, and the sad cycle of teacher's threat and student's resentment has been launched. It is not uncommon to find entire classrooms caught up in this unfortunate circle with the likely spin-off of tension and discipline problems. In this manner the infrequent use of threat can be a deterrent to a positive motivational climate. See Figure 1.

Myth 5: *Learning automatically improves with increased student motivation.* There is no conclusive evidence to support the intuitive notion that motivation enhances learning. The effects of student motivation depend on the type of learning (learning to read vs. learning to write), the type of task (verbal, nonverbal, simple, complex, etc.), the cognitive style of the learner (audial, visual, tactile, etc.), and the type of setting (group or individual), as well as other factors. Students also do not learn in an even, linear fashion. There are many peaks, valleys, and plateaus. At this time, motivation appears to be a necessary, but not a sufficient, condition for learning.

What this means is that "laziness" and apathy do not account for all problems in learning; they are simplistic excuses with little value for the teacher. We need to look more at the process and performance of our students and less at the more narrow and self-defeating emphasis of product or acquisition. If a student is responding with enthusiasm and interest, she/he will probably learn, but often without a neat, continuous, daily progress line. To lose our students' excitement and involvement for lack of immediate learning is not only a waste of effort but also a danger to the ultimate goal of any teacher—a student who is on the road to becoming a lifelong learner.

Figure 1

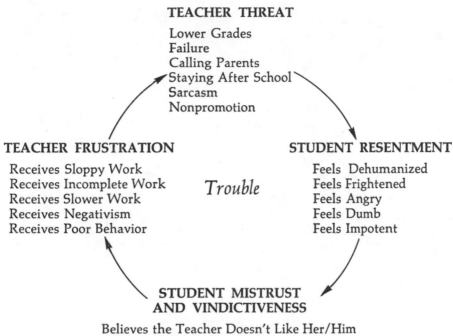

TEACHER THREAT

Lower Grades
Failure
Calling Parents
Staying After School
Sarcasm
Nonpromotion

TEACHER FRUSTRATION

Receives Sloppy Work
Receives Incomplete Work
Receives Slower Work
Receives Negativism
Receives Poor Behavior

Trouble

STUDENT RESENTMENT

Feels Dehumanized
Feels Frightened
Feels Angry
Feels Dumb
Feels Impotent

**STUDENT MISTRUST
AND VINDICTIVENESS**

Believes the Teacher Doesn't Like Her/Him
Believes the Teacher Is Unfair
Believes the Teacher Is Mean
Believes the Teacher Doesn't Understand
Believes She/He Should Get Even

The Time Continuum Model of Motivation

Until now we have talked about what motivation is, what its various components appear to be, how it relates to learning, and some popular misconceptions about motivation. With this section we shall concentrate on the practical and useful employment of knowledge about motivation to enhance our teaching and to facilitate the learning of our students. The main questions that should follow every page for the reader are, "How does this apply to me?" and, "How can I use this?"

The key ingredient in the successful use of what follows is *planning*. I believe that motivation is a complex and ambiguous concept, but that we have much knowledge in the field that can be applied in a logical and effective manner. It is how we apply and organize this knowledge that can make a difference. Just as we plan lessons and organize objectives, we need to plan our motivation strategies. If we want to enhance our students' motivation, we must think about those methods and techniques that will be effective. We can still be spontaneous, but within a structure of approaches that has the highest probability of facilitating motivation. This is an evolving task that takes reflection and proper analysis. It is not something we can do continuously "off the cuff" or without careful consideration. Even those of you who teach successfully without ever planning for motivation are doing something that relates to what will follow.

I have written this book with one guiding idea—*effective teachers do not need to threaten or coerce their students*. There is a myriad of things that can be done in order to facilitate motivation. There is no joy in teaching when there is threat. The love of learning is not a Utopian idea. It is a reality in the relationship of an effective teacher and a responsible student.

Every learning situation, whether it lasts 10 minutes or 10 days, can be divided according to a time continuum. There is always a beginning, a middle, and an end. There are effective things that can be done during each of these phases to facilitate motivation. Each phase has a maximum potential for the employment of motivational methods that can optimally influence the learner's motivation. Each phase also relates to the others in forming a dynamic whole that, when proper motivation strategies are applied according to their particular phase, enhances the overall learning experience and catalyzes the students' positive return to the learning situation.

Another way of describing this phenomenon is that there are three critical periods in any learning event during which particular motivation strategies will have maximum impact on the learner's motivation. These are:

1. *Beginning*—when the student enters and starts the learning process.

2. *During*—when the student is involved in the body or main content of the learning process.

3. *Ending*—when the student is finishing or completing the learning process.

For each of the above critical periods, there are two general motivational factors that serve as categories for strategies that can be applied with maximum impact during those periods of time. They are:

Beginning: 1. *Attitude*—the student's attitude toward the general learning environment, teacher, subject matter, and self.
2. *Needs*—the basic needs within the student at the time of learning.

During: 1. *Stimulation*—the stimulation process affecting the student via the learning experience.
2. *Affect*—the affective or emotional experience of the student while learning.

Ending: 1. *Competence*—the competence value for the student that is a result of the learning behavior.
2. *Reinforcement*—the reinforcement value attached to the learning experience for the student.

Each of the above six factors can be understood or evaluated by the teacher to some degree in order to facilitate student motivation, prevent motivation problems, and diagnose motivation potential in learning situations.

Using a math course as an example (see Figure 2), a student may have a poor history of success in mathematics with related low grades and, therefore, have a very poor *attitude* toward the subject matter. However, this same student may *need* math in order to graduate and, therefore, feel some sense of determination to "get through it." Thus, at the beginning of the math course, we have a student who is not very enthusiastic but who is willing to "give it a try." If the teacher can provide math problems and exercises that are interesting and relevant to the student, she/he may find math *stimulating* and attempt to do well. If the student also enjoys her/his classmates and works with them toward solving mutual problems, the student may actually be further motivated by the *affective* climate in the classroom. Toward the end of the course, the student's mastery of the math skills may give her/him a feeling of confidence and *competence,* but if the student fails the final exam and receives a low grade, she/he will not feel *reinforced*, and it is unlikely that the student will continue her/his interest in math in the future. This example serves to illustrate how the six general motivation factors interact on a dynamic basis to impede or facilitate student motivation along a time continuum.

Figure 2

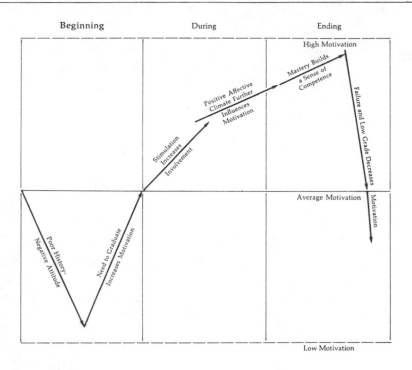

The model in Figure 3 graphically indicates the general categorization, relationships, and influences on motivation of these six factors.

Although each general motivation factor has been indicated as separate, there is some degree of overlap among them—i.e., needs in part determine attitudes, competence can be viewed as reinforcing, etc. They represent an eclectic view toward motivation with an emphasis on the phenomenological viewpoint of the student. Each factor should be considered in the overall motivational plan of the teacher. Some teachers may choose to put their emphasis on meeting the needs of the learner, while others may focus more of their energies on making the learning process as stimulating as possible, but neither group would be wise to disregard the other factors.

It is very important to note that the motivational model in Figure 3 is based on a time continuum. Thus, the learner's motivation with respect to needs and attitudes is modified by past experience but it exerts a present influence as she/he begins the learning process. These

Figure 3

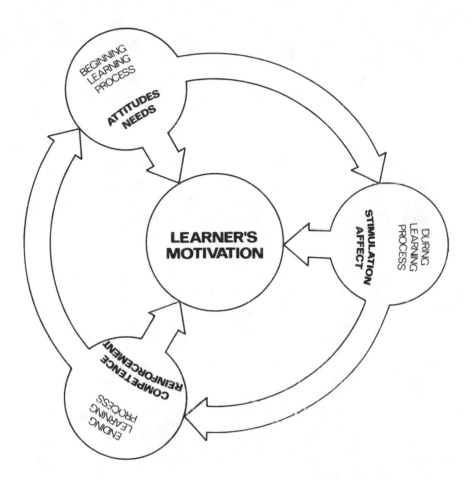

needs and attitudes combine to interact with stimulation and the affective processes of the learning experience itself to further influence motivation as it occurs during learning. At the end of the learning process, the competence value and the reinforcement gained interact with the previous four factors to influence the learner's motivation at that moment, and for the future as well, resulting in new attitudes and needs. Although the motivational influence is shown in three separate phases, in reality, it is constantly interacting with the learner.

Some Case Illustrations

Each motivation factor has its own degree of potency in influencing motivation in a particular learning situation. Any of the six identified factors can be so powerful as to prevent any involvement in learning or, on the other hand, so strong as to produce a desire to learn that overrides the possible negative influence of the other five factors. For example, some student attitudes are so negative toward a particular teacher that even though they need the course, are confronted with stimulating materials, have good friends in the class, can master the necessary skills, and know they can receive a good grade with minimal effort, they refuse to try to learn. On the other hand, a student's felt need for a degree can be so strong that she/he takes subjects for which she/he feels no practical use, suffers through boring teachers in classes dominated by feelings of alienation and loneliness, and survives with little sense of accomplishment or mastery. Although these two examples are not common, they are by no means rare.

Each motivation factor also appears to have the potential (for good or bad) to undermine the factors which precede it. As an undergraduate in college, I avoided physical science courses at all costs. However, I was informed in my senior year that I could not graduate without one. I approached this dilemma with astute logical questioning. I asked my college friends two questions. First, which was the easiest physical science course? And secondly, who was the easiest instructor for that course? The criterion in both instances was, How could I receive the best grade for the least amount of work? The consensus of opinion was that I wanted to take Geology 101 as taught by Hildinbiddle.

My attitude toward the class was reflected by the fact that on the first day of class I sat in the last seat in the last row with my arms folded and my fists clenched. When Hildinbiddle entered the room, he handed each of us a small box with 24 rocks in it. I remember muttering something about throwing them, but when I opened the carton, I was unexpectedly surprised. They were colorful, different, and unusual. We immediately began short and interesting experiments to test their hardness and cleavage. I found myself magnetically involved. This continued with the addition of field trips to sandstone and shale quarries (I even found a trilobite) that were social fun as well as scientifically interesting. Within eight weeks I wanted to be a geologist.

I received a high grade for the course and enrolled in Geology 102. The stimulation of this course had countered the very negative attitudes which initially dominated my feelings upon entering the class. (I dropped Geology 102 in three weeks. It turned out to be what I thought the first course would be—boring and difficult.)

This anecdote serves to emphasize the potency that an individual motivation factor, namely stimulation, can possess. However, in most instances, the motivation factors are more equal in their particular influence and should be individually considered and planned for in any teaching situation. The most productive route is to plan strategies for each factor so that a continuous and interactive motivational dynamic is organized for maximum effective teaching. Therefore, there are six basic questions to be considered by the teacher in the planning of any learning experience:

1. What can I do to guarantee a positive student attitude for this activity?
2. How do I best meet the needs of my students through this activity?
3. What about this activity will continuously stimulate my students?
4. How is the affective or emotional climate for this activity a positive one for students?
5. How does this activity increase or affirm student feelings of competence?
6. What is the reinforcement that this activity provides for my students?

If each of these questions is adequately answered and integrated into the learning experience, students will have an excellent chance of being motivated to learn.

The primary value of the model presented in Figure 3 is that it is an organizational aid. It can be applied to groups or to individuals. By continuously attending to the six factors outlined, the teacher can, in any learning situation, design motivation strategies for her/his students throughout the learning process. Each general factor has been chosen for its logical practicality and application. The general factors can be subdivided according to more specific categories with accompanying diagnostic questions and motivation strategies. These are found in the Diagnostic Motivation Chart in Figure 4.

Figure 4

DIAGNOSTIC MOTIVATION CHART

Motivation Factors	Diagnostic Questions	Motivation Strategies

Attitudes

Attitude toward the teacher	What are the student's perceptions and feelings toward the teacher?	1. Establish a relationship with the student by sharing something of value with the student. 2. Listen to the student with empathetic regard. 3. Treat the student with warmth and acceptance. 4. Use class or individual meetings to build relationships and better attitudes.
Attitude toward the subject and learning situation	What are the student's perceptions and feelings toward the subject and the learning situation?	1. Make the conditions that surround the subject positive. 2. Model enthusiasm for the subject taught. 3. Associate the student with other students who are enthusiastic about the subject. 4. Positively confront the possible erroneous beliefs, expectations, and assumptions that may underly the negative student attitude. 5. Make the first experience with the subject matter as positive as possible.

Motivation Factors	Diagnostic Questions	Motivation Strategies
Attitude toward the self	What are the student's sense of worth and capabilities in the learning situation?	1. Guarantee successful learning. 2. Encourage the student. 3. Emphasize the student's personal causation in learning. 4. Use group process methods to enhance a positive self-concept in the student.
Expectancy for success	How well does the student honestly and objectively expect to do in the learning situation?	1. Interview the student. 2. Use goal-setting methods. 3. Use contracting methods. 4. Use programmed materials.

Needs

Physiological needs	What is the condition of the student's physical well being?	1. When relevant, select content, examples, and projects that relate to the physiological needs of the students. 2. Be alert to restlessness in students and relieve the causes producing it.
Safety needs	How is the learning situation free of fear and threat?	1. When relevant, select content, examples, and projects that relate to the safety needs of the students. 2. Reduce or remove components of the learning environment that lead to failure or fear.

Motivation Factors	*Diagnostic Questions*	Motivation Strategies
		3. Create a learning environment that is organized and orderly.
		4. Don't expect initiative and self-discipline from insecure students.
		5. Introduce the unfamiliar through the familiar.
Belongingness and love needs	How does the student have a sense of acceptance and belonging in the learning situation?	1. When relevant, select content, examples, and projects that relate to the belongingness and love needs of the students.
		2. Increase or create components in the learning environment that tell the student that she/he is wanted and that significant others care about her or him.
		3. Devise a system by which duties and responsibilities are designated in such a way that all students become functioning members of the group.
Esteem needs	How does the learning activity promote the student's self-respect?	1. Offer the opportunity for responsible attainment of learning goals that affirm the student's identity or role.
		2. Offer students subject matter, assignments, and learning modes that appeal to and complement their strengths and assets.
		3. Offer subject matter in such a way that it enhances the student's independence as a learner and as a person.

Motivation Factors	Diagnostic Questions	Motivation Strategies
		4. Plan activities to allow students to publicly display and share their talents and work.
Self-actualization needs	How does the student exercise full potential in the learning situation?	1. Provide students with the opportunity to select topics, projects, and assignments that appeal to their curiosity, sense of wonder, and need to explore.
		2. Encourage divergent thinking and creativity in the learning process.
		3. Provide the opportunity for self-discovery through freedom of choice in the learning situation with emphasis on risk taking, problem solving, experimentation, and self-evaluation.

Stimulation

Motivation Factors	Diagnostic Questions	Motivation Strategies
Introduction and connection of learning activities	How are the various subtopics and sub-units of learning effectively introduced and connected?	1. Use focusing methods and/or materials to draw student attention to the new learning activity or topic.
		2. For recitation and discussion, use Kounin's positive group alerting cues.
Variety	What is there that is continually different about the learner's environment and activities?	1. Whenever possible, let the learner control the pace, choices, and changes in the learning activity.
		2. Use movement, voice, body language, pauses, and props to vitalize and accentuate classroom presentations.

Motivation Factors	Diagnostic Questions	Motivation Strategies
		3. Shift interaction between yourself and the students and between the students themselves during classroom presentations.
		4. Change the style as well as the content of the learning activities.
		5. Use closure techniques to help students organize their attention to the end of a topic or subunit of learning.
Interest and involvement	How does the learner figuratively step into and become a part of the learning activity? Can the student escape by not paying attention?	1. Guarantee success and pleasure at the beginning of any new learning experience.
		2. Find out student interests and relate learning to them.
		3. Use humor, examples, analogies, stories, and questions to facilitate the active participation of students in your lectures and demonstrations.
		4. Whenever possible, make student reaction and involvement essential parts of the learning process—i.e., problem solving, games, role playing, simulation, etc.
Questions	In the learner's perception, how stimulating and provocative are the questions being discussed?	1. Limit the use of knowledge questions, and selectively increase the use of comprehension, application, analysis, synthesis, and evaluation questions.
		2. Employ M. Sadker and D. Sadker's suggestions for improving the quality of questioning skills that enhance student responsiveness.

Motivation Factors	Diagnostic Questions	Motivation Strategies
Disequilibrium	How is the learner confronted with information or processes that are different, novel, contrasting, or discrepant from what she/he already knows or has experienced?	1. Introduce contrasting or disturbing data and information. 2. Permit a humane degree of student mistakes and frustrations. 3. Play the devil's advocate. 4. Facilitate the search and recognition of incomplete Gestalts. 5. Be unpredictable to the degree that students enjoy your spontaneity with a sense of security.
Affect		
Feelings	How does the learner feel about how and what she/he is learning?	1. When emotions are apparent, recognize and accept the student's feelings. 2. When there are strong feelings, possible misunderstandings, and/or conflicts between yourself and a student, paraphrase her or his message to continue communication and show understanding. 3. When a student seems unmotivated, simply describe her/his behavior and ask an open-ended question to facilitate understanding and resolution of the issue. 4. Whenever a student's feelings seem relevant but are unstated or ambiguous, check your impression of them to open communication and facilitate motivation.

Motivation Factors	Diagnostic Questions	Motivation Strategies
		5. Directly describe your feelings to resolve problems with a student and to avoid continual anger and resentment.
Confluency	How does what the student is learning relate to what she/he feels now and believes is important or of real concern to her or his daily life?	1. Have the student "live out" the cognitive concepts presented by experiencing them in the classroom setting. 2. Have the student imagine and deal with learning experiences as they relate to her/his real life. 3. Use student concerns to organize content and to develop themes and teaching procedures.
Valuing	How does what the student is learning relate to what she/he values?	1. Use values clarification methods and activities to facilitate learning.
Climate	How does the learner experience the learning environment in terms of group cohesion, personal acceptance, open communication, and cooperation?	1. Use Gibb's supportive communication behaviors to facilitate a positive climate. 2. Use a cooperative goal structure to maximize student involvement and sharing. 3. Make group decisions by consensus. 4. For problems with a student or group of students, use Gordon's Conflict Resolution Model. 5. Use "climate surveys" to diagnose your classroom atmosphere.

Motivation Factors	Diagnostic Questions	Motivation Strategies
		6. Use self-diagnostic questioning procedures to reflect upon how your behavior influences the classroom atmosphere.

Competence

Motivation Factors	Diagnostic Questions	Motivation Strategies
Awareness of progress and mastery	How does the student know that she/he is effectively learning and can use this learning to cope with important or new environments?	1. Provide consistent feedback regarding mastery of learning. 2. Use constructive criticism. 3. Facilitate successful completion of the agreed-upon learning task. 4. Help the learner to realize how to operationalize in daily living what has been learned.
Responsibility	How is the student aware at the completion of learning that she/he has "personally caused" and is accountable for that learning?	1. Acknowledge and affirm the student's responsibility in completing the learning task. 2. Use a competence checklist for student self-rating. 3. Acknowledge the risk taking and challenge involved in the learning accomplishment.

Reinforcement

Motivation Factors	Diagnostic Questions	Motivation Strategies
Artificial reinforcers	How is student motivation facilitated by being concretely rewarded at the end of the learning behavior?	1. When any subject matter or learning activity is so aversive that the five other general motivation factors cannot facilitate student motivation, artificial reinforcers may be initially employed.

Motivation Factors	*Diagnostic* Questions	Motivation Strategies
		2. Provide artificial reinforcers when they contribute to the natural flow of successful learning and provide closure with a positive ending.
Natural consequences	How does the student realize learning intrinsically produces changes that are positive and desirable?	1. When learning has natural consequences, allow them to be congruently evident.
Grades	How does the grading procedure facilitate and support student motivation?	1. Do not use traditional grades as the only form of feedback on student work. 2. Discuss with and involve your students in the grading procedure you intend to employ. 3. Use student self-evaluation as part of your grading decision. 4. Do not grade on a normal curve. 5. Have your grading process supportive of your teaching style.

This chart is divided into three basic areas: motivation factors, diagnostic questions, and motivation strategies. Each motivation factor is a subfactor or specific categorization of the six general factors— e.g., under the general factor of attitudes, we have the subfactors of attitude toward the teacher, attitude toward the subject and learning situation, and attitude toward self and expectancy for success. Each of these subfactors has been chosen for its concrete practical value as an apparent influence on student motivation. In the case of attitudes, students have attitudes toward the teacher and the learning situation as well as toward themselves, and each of these combines with others to influence student motivation in terms of starting, continuing, and finishing learning activities.

The six general factors serve as "windows of reality" by which we can view student motivation. We can see student behavior as a result of student attitudes and make our plans accordingly. We can also perceive student behavior as a result of the stimulation value of a particular learning activity and organize our lessons with this viewpoint in mind. Both approaches may satisfactorily help us facilitate student motivation.

In certain instances it might be more helpful to use an attitudinal approach than to use an entire plan based on theories of stimulation. An example of this might be a learning situation in which most of the students seem to be having fun and enjoying the activity while one student remains turned-off and negative. Her/his problem may be better explained by attitudinal theory.

It is important to note that entire motivation theories could be built around any one of the six general factors. However, I have never found that a single general factor or window of reality answered all the questions I had or was so thoroughly useful as to exclude the possible advantages of perceiving the learning situation through the use of the other general factors or windows of reality. What I have found is that particular general factors seem to serve to their greatest advantage when employed according to a time line which divides a learning experience into a beginning (attitude and need), a middle (stimulation and affect), and an end (competence and reinforcement).

This has led me to a "leave no stone unturned" approach to motivation. That is, each of the six general factors should be considered and utilized for the advantages it offers to the teachers at a certain point in time when conducting a learning experience for students. Just as in driving a car, when we use the front window, we also need at times to use the rear view mirror as well as the side windows and side mirrors. It is only very rarely that we might complete a trip without full employment of all windows and mirrors while we travel to our destination.

How much to use any single general factor is a vital question. This will remain unique and vary according to the teacher, student, and learning situation. Some of us, by virtue of values, experience, and talent, may choose those motivation factors which best suit our beliefs, abilities, and situation. An insightful analogy for this is to see student motivation and teaching as a musical arrangement. Each general factor represents a series of notes that may be played relative to our talent and taste. How often and in what pattern we (teachers) select these notes (general and specific factors) will result in a certain melody (student motivation) that we may care to play again or to alter depending on its results. There are many different melodies as well as types of music. To me, this is the art of teaching. In many ways the manner in which we conduct a class is a melody or simply a chaotic series of sounds. But we must have technique (motivation strategies) and knowledge (motivation theory) to advance music as well as the art of teaching. Each of the following chapters in this book centers on a general motivation factor and its specific subfactors. Your values, experience, and situation will determine how you can relate them to your profession. Just as perfect music does not exist, I do not believe that perfect teaching exists. We select those motivation strategies that we enjoy and desire, just as we select music on much the same basis.

With each specific motivation subfactor is a correlated diagnostic question (see Figure 4); e.g., expectancy for success—How well does the student honestly and objectively expect to do in the learning situation? Such questions are intended to help us more accurately perceive motivational influences upon the learner. If the motivational influences appear to be lacking, absent, or nonfunctioning, there are a number of correlated strategies that can be employed to facilitate the learner's motivation. For example, if the learner does not honestly and objectively expect to do well in the learning situation, the teacher might use a contracting system or a goal-setting strategy or programmed materials to more positively influence the student's motivation. The diagnostic question helps to identify the malfunctioning factor and suggests appropriate motivation strategies that indicate what to do to assist a poorly motivated student or to prevent a motivation problem from occurring.

To my knowledge there is no measure or test of motivation that prescribes what teacher behaviors should be in order to prevent or reduce motivation problems. Because motivation is so complex, there may never be such an instrument.

Using the diagnostic questions, we can find motivation strategies regarding *what to do*. However, these strategies are not perfect solutions. They are realistic methods or techniques that have a logical probability of being helpful to the teacher and the student. *How they are employed is the crucial question.* Extensive discussion of how to utilize each strategy is contained in the following chapters where the general and specific motivation factors are combined with their most productive strategies.

Chapter 2   **Attitudes:**
Perceptions and
Judgments that
Influence Action

Attitudes are powerful. They have pushbutton efficiency with long-term effects on human behavior. Technically they are the combination of a perception with a judgment that often results in an emotion that influences behavior. See Figure 5.

Figure 5

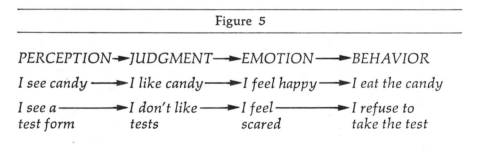

PERCEPTION→JUDGMENT──→EMOTION──→BEHAVIOR

I see candy ──→ I like candy──→I feel happy──→I eat the candy

I see a──────→I don't like──→I feel──────→I refuse to
test form   tests   scared   take the test

Attitudes are usually based on beliefs that are learned and that result from experience. A young child who enters kindergarten sees her/his teacher for the first time. The teacher is a person who reminds the child of one of her/his parents. The child loves her/his parents, and, therefore, likes the teacher and feels safe in her/his company. The child wants to please the teacher and is motivated to learn because of this. On the other hand, a 13-year-old student has heard from a friend that her/his new teacher is mean and unfair. During her/his first class with the teacher, the teacher, in a matter-of-fact manner, discusses the course and its requirements. The student judges the teacher's objective style to be cold and hostile. She/he fears the teacher and wants to drop the class.

Both of these examples reflect attitudes and how they influence behavior. Attitudes receive much of their power because they help students to make sense of their world and give cues as to what behavior will be most effective in dealing with what world. If someone is going to be hostile, it is in our best interest to be careful of, and even to withdraw from, that person. Attitudes allow students to feel psychologically safe around subjects and teachers that are initially unknown to them.

Although sometimes self-defeating, attitudes usually give us a sense that we are in control of our environment. Because of a particular attitude, we feel we can predict the situation and, therefore, make the responses that will best help us. In many instances we are not even aware of the belief or previous experience that has led to our present attitude. In this manner, attitudes are most difficult to challenge or change. And if they are well learned, they will be even more difficult to alter. (A fifth-grade student is about to begin a new spelling lesson. For the past three years this student has never received a grade in spelling that has been higher than a "C." For her/him to be enthusiastic about this spelling lesson would be irrational. The student has very little reason from past experience to believe that she/he is going to do well. To be very positively excited about the lesson may only act to heighten her/his disappointment and regret about doing poorly. So, to protect herself/himself, the student apathetically responds to the lesson. A teacher's comment such as, "This is going to be fun," may do very little to change this attitude. A positive attitude on the part of the teacher seldom hurts, but in this situation, it may not help. The student may only resist further to reduce potential personal feelings of disappointment.)

Attitudes are attitudes, and they may be helpful or harmful for the student. Attitudes helpful from a teacher's viewpoint are those that enable a student to learn, grow, and flourish. They lead to satisfaction and joy. Harmful attitudes are those that cause a student to be self-defeating and that decrease her/his growth and abilities. They lead to negative and self-destructive forms of behavior. A bad attitude toward oneself, a poor attitude toward a teacher without sufficient reason, and a low expectancy for success are often inappropriate attitudes that continue cycles of cynicism and self-defeat. We will now take a more careful look at attitudes and related methods to change or enhance them.

Attitude Toward the Teacher

If a student likes a teacher and feels that the teacher is a fair, warm, and caring person, the student's motivation to learn should be enhanced. In addition it is quite likely that under these conditions, the student might identify with the teacher and be likely to imitate the teacher's behavior and style. However, when a student does not like the teacher and feels hostile, fearful, or dehumanized by the teacher, that student's motivation to learn is seriously impaired. Under such conditions, the teacher is literally a barrier between the student and the subject matter. When we do not like someone, we experience dissonance (unpleasant psychological tension) when we find out that they like something we like. One of the easiest ways to relieve that tension is to reduce our liking for that something. The same is true for the student. She/he may wonder, "How could I be interested in such a subject if a lousy teacher like this is interested in it?" Instead of having the "touch of gold," such a teacher in the student's view-point has the "touch of doom." Things liked, proposed, or advocated by such a teacher are guilty by association and are rejected by the student, often without reason or forethought. Students who don't like their teachers are programmed to resist, rebel, disrupt, and subvert the learning goals of their teachers.

It is important to note that, in many instances, we as teachers have not directly evoked these reactions. They often occur as a result of what we symbolize, what we represent.

Pain and confusion can result for the recipient of unprovoked negative student attitudes. In this regard, we are unable to change the past, but we can do much to resolve the present and improve the future.

Strategy 1: *Establish a relationship with the student by sharing something of value with the student.* Whenever a student has a nega-tive attitude toward us,[1] she/he usually attempts to remain at a psychological distance from us. The student's rationale for this be-havior is usually fear or hostility. Because the student has little contact with us, she/he can easily maintain or support this position by continuing this distance through labeling us as mean, cold, unfair, prejudiced, etc. In many ways, we become a caricature to the student because this student does not have any direct contact with us to alter those opinions and to help her/him see us as human beings. Sharing is a positive way to reduce that distance and bring the student into contact with our own humanity. It allows the student to perceive us as "givers" instead of as "takers," to view us as persons beyond a specified school role and as persons with feelings of joy and compassion. Otherwise, we can be easily cast by the student into an image of repression and control.

What we share is important. We can begin by sharing *time*. By giving a student *individual attention,* we tell the student that we regard her/him as someone special. The quality of the time should be positive and helpful. This can take many different forms: a few minutes in class, lunch together, a talk after school, or even an outing. This can be an initial step in breaking the spiral of hostility and distance between ourselves and rejecting students.

We can also share *humor.* Most professional speakers at banquets and meetings begin their presentations with a joke or a humorous story. They do this because it's positive, it breaks the tensions, and it tells the listeners that the speaker has emotions and feelings—that the speaker is human. Essentially the message is that if we can laugh together, we can enjoy each other and learn together. The basic question for us then is, Does the student see our lighter side? Or are we always serious . . . deadly serious?

We can share *our feelings and values.* To our students some of us appear to be robot-like dispensers of information and control. To let students know spontaneously and tactfully about the things we cherish, without lecturing or demanding similar feelings from them, is a way to convey our humanity. I have always been sadly amazed at the way students ridicule teachers who cry in class. Perhaps this has been because such reactions usually come at a time of chaotic disorder and frustration. But it is also an indictment of the emotional vacuum that schools perpetuate. The classroom is a legitimate place for the expression of our joy and our sadness when events deserving of such emotions take place.

We can share *something about our real selves.* Teachers do much more than just teach. Yet students continue to be amazed by this. A story I once heard from an actress on a talk show illustrates this. She was telling the emcee how as a child she had been shocked by seeing her teacher in a supermarket. She recounted how she was left speechless by seeing her teacher push a cart and actually smell the melons and squeeze the oranges! She mentioned how her relationship to that teacher had been irrevocably changed by witnessing "grocery store behavior." In some ways, this is a funny story, but it also points out how confining the teacher's role is if we let it be that. Self-disclosure to students seems especially effective when we reveal common experiences that they are currently relating to such as television shows, sports, travel, first experiences, and maybe even a little trouble we've had with life along the way. The criteria for revealing ourselves are always good taste and proper timing. Ego trips may take us a long way, but leave our students behind.

Concrete rewards are means by which we share our sense of caring for students. A spontaneous treat, free tickets to a valued show or sporting event, demonstrations of hobbies or collections (records, stamps, etc.), guest speakers, desired field trips, lending personal equipment, etc., are all ways of saying to the student, "I like you and want you to enjoy." I have left this suggestion until last because there is the possible implication of "buying affection." However, if this means is used with good judgment and in the context of the other suggestions in this section, it has little chance of being manipulative or abused.

A final word about sharing—it is always a risk. Negative students can reject or abuse what we offer. However, we cannot wait for them to take the first step. Any relationship demands a certain degree of vulnerability for trust to be established. There is an old cliché: "You have to give in order to get." As with all clichés, this is a bit of truth quoted to the point of satiation. Yet its meaning stands firm. Until we change, our students stand little chance of changing themselves.

Strategy 2: *Listen to the student with empathetic regard.* Our goal here is to communicate to the student that *we want to understand the situation as the student perceives it* and that *we are accurate in our awareness of her/his message.* Listening with understanding is one basic way to show a student respect and caring. If we do this with skill and feeling, the student cannot easily walk away with the impression that we don't care or that we only want to control the situation.

An effective way to do this is to rephrase in our own words the gist of the student's expression without changing the meaning or the emotional tone of the student. This means that we do not interrupt, evaluate, add to, or lessen the meaning of the message we receive. For example:

Student: "I can't stand the way you treat me. You're trying to push me around and make me do everything just the way you want it."

Teacher: "You think I'm bullying and forcing you to behave my way and are upset by it."

Student: "Yes, it happens whenever . . . ."

This is just a short example of listening with empathetic regard. Entire books have been written on this topic,[2] and you may wish to refer to them for greater skill building. The main goal is to break the cycle of negative student attitudes toward ourselves in our daily communication with students through empathetic listening behavior. The way we listen is a consistent and pervasive influence on our students that can, at best, positively influence their motivation or, at worst, subvert our best intentions.

Strategy 3: *Treat the student with warmth and acceptance*. It's very difficult to continue to dislike someone who genuinely and consistently appears to like you. A student with a negative attitude toward us is programmed to interpret our behavior as cold and rejecting. When we consistently show acceptance and warmth toward the student, we frustrate the student's expectancy which may lead to dissonance and provide the opportunity for a positive change in that attitude toward us.

Acceptance is any behavior toward a student which indicates to the student that she/he is a worthwhile person in her/his own right. The following list of behaviors indicates ways to demonstrate acceptance:

1. Making any statement that essentially tells the student that she/he is a worthwhile person.

2. Being available.

3. Being helpful.

4. Being supportive.

5. Asking the student for help.

6. Showing understanding.

7. Showing caring or liking.

8. Taking the student seriously.

9. Self-disclosing to the student.

10. Sharing with the student.

11. Encouraging the student.

12. Allowing the student opportunity for expression.

13. Allowing the student freedom of expression.

Warmth, the *necessary* nonverbal counterpart to acceptance, is the positive way or manner of the teacher's expression which displays its genuine quality. Some of the nonverbal cues that indicate warmth are:

1. *Tone of voice*—soft, pleasant, expressive, etc.

2. *Facial expression*—smiling, interested, appropriately intense, etc.

3. *Posture*—leaning toward, relaxed, open, etc.

4. *Eye contact*—looking into the student's eyes.

5. *Touching*—gentle, embracing, supportive, etc.

6. *Gestures*—welcoming, beckoning, stroking, etc.

7. *Spatial distance*—appropriately close.

When we are authentically warm and accepting toward our students, there is little chance of overusing this strategy. The trick is not to expect it back until trust reaches a level where reciprocity is possible. Otherwise, it can become manipulative and guilt-provoking for the student, and unnecessarily frustrating for us.

Strategy 4: *Use class or individual meetings to build relationships and better attitudes.* In many instances, more than one student may have a negative attitude toward us. Sometime it's just a few, and at times it may even be a majority of the class. In both situations, a class meeting to prevent or resolve this problem may be useful.[3] The purpose of this meeting is to take a problem-solving approach[4] in which there is a nonpunitive and a nonjudgmental climate with emphasis on individual and group responsibility for positive class relationships. As the teacher, you will set the tone for the meeting by your own self-disclosure and openness to change. Some guidelines for this are:

1. Describe how the negative attitude *involves* you.

2. Discuss how you *feel* and *react* in this situation.

3. Acknowledge how *you might create or continue* the negative attitudes.

4. Describe *what you want* as a result of the meeting.

For example: "Class, I want to talk with you about a problem I've been having with some members of our group. (1) I don't think I've been getting along with some of you very well lately. I'm fairly sure this involves Jack, Shirley, and Jan, but there may be a few more. It seems to me that hard feelings have resulted from homework and grading procedures. (2) I know I'm feeling tense and have been demanding with you on these things. (3) I sense that I might be pushing you too hard or asking for too much, but I'm not sure. (4) I'd like to discuss this with all of you and get your opinions and feedback so we can resolve this problem. . . ."

The advantages of the class-meeting approach are many. It gives the opportunity for other phenomenological views to be expressed. Most students have some members of their reference group in the class and will use them as standards by which to judge and evaluate their attitudes. They, as well as we, can receive concrete feedback which has a real probability of changing attitudes. This procedure also prevents *insulated ignorance* which is the protection of sensitive attitudes by not showing them or hearing other opinions regarding them. For any of this to work, we must be willing to change ourselves. If not, this group process is only a manipulation.

The same approach can be used on an individual basis. Again, the four criteria outlined above are important for the initiation and overall discussion of the issue. To illustrate: (1) "Bart, I have not felt comfortable with our work together. (2) I don't think I'm communicating with you, and I feel tense and easily frustrated when I help you. (3) I think it might have something to do with the grade I gave you on your last report card. (4) I don't want to have a bad relationship with you, and I would like to hear what you think and feel so we can work this out. . . ."

Both class and individual meetings to deal with relationships are risks for us. We can get severe criticism and may need to change. Some students will not trust us enough to reveal their thoughts or feelings. Timing is important to consider. If we can take these risks without expecting conclusive results, we stand little chance of hurting our students and a good chance of opening the door to better student motivation.

Attitude Toward the Subject and Learning Situation

"I can't stand English."

"If I ever have to do another math problem, I'll die."

"Social studies is the living death."

"I love to write."

"Math really turns me on."

"This social studies is fun."

These are common expressions heard in all schools. All of them reflect an attitude. When students like what they're learning, the classroom is filled with the two -isms of motivation—optimism and enthusiasm. The students are hopeful, cheerful, and confident. We are in gear. The mental set behind the students' perception is to accept, to be involved, and to persevere.

When students dislike what they're learning, the classroom is filled with the two -isms of apathy—pessimism and cynicism. The students are despondent, gloomy, and angry. We are defensive and strained. There is stress in the air. The mental set behind the students' perception is to reject, to be distracted, and to self-destruct or *cut out*.

We know our subject is a worthy one. We want to convince the students. We want to make them into believers. But, as Mager has written, "Exhortation is used more and accomplishes less than almost any behavior-changing tool known to man."[5] It still comes down to what we are going to *do*. Here are some realistic possibilities.

Strategy 1: *Make the conditions that surround the subject positive.*[6] It is a common fact of learning that when a person is presented with an item or subject, and is at the same time in the presence of positive (pleasant) conditions, that item or subject becomes a stimulus for approach behavior. Our favorite things and subjects are often associated with good friends, caring relatives, excellent teachers, and comfort and satisfaction. Things or subjects that frighten us are just as often associated with antagonists and situations that make us uncomfortable and tense. Therefore, avoid associating your subject with any of the following conditions that tend to support negative attitudes and repel student interest:

44

1. *Pain*—acute physical or psychological discomfort, i.e., punishment, failure, poorly fitting equipment, etc.

2. *Fear and anxiety*—distress and tension resulting from anticipation of the unpleasant or dangerous, i.e., threat of failure or punishment, public exposure of ignorance, unpredictability of potential negative consequences, etc.

3. *Frustration*—an emotional reaction to blockage or defeat of purposeful behavior, i.e., presenting information too fast or too slowly, an unannounced test, inadequate feedback on performance, etc.

4. *Humiliation*—an emotional reaction to being shamed, debased, or degraded, i.e., sarcasm, insult, public comparison of inadequate learning, repeated failure, etc.

5. *Boredom*—a cognitive and emotional reaction to a situation in which stimuli impinging on the student are weak, repetitive, or infrequent, i.e., lack of variety, covering material already known, continuously reading out loud, predictable discussion issues, etc.

Increase the association of your subject matter with conditions that lead to student awareness of success, stimulating experiences, and increased confidence and self-esteem.[7]

Strategy 2: *Model enthusiasm for the subject taught.* One of the basic motivational questions that any student asks about a subject is, "What can learning this do for me?" The question is usually not asked out loud. In fact, the answer is generally inferred from another question that goes something like this: "What does teaching this subject do for my teacher?" If we appear bored, listless, and "burned out" by what we teach, we have little chance of influencing any positive attitude change in our students.

We mirror the soul of our subject matter. In many ways, we are the living extension of the benefits of knowing and appreciating what we teach. If it hasn't been good for us and we have spent our lives learning it in order to teach it, any sensitive student will turn away before being victimized as well. How good we feel about what we teach is the greatest advocacy for it. *Enthusiasm* is the popular term given when our students feel it in us. All people are attracted by life. There is a magnetic pull to know and understand what gives energy to the spirited teacher.

How do we model enthusiasm?

1. *By dramatizing what we know*—telling interesting stories about what we teach; acting out the process of the subject (history teachers become historical figures, English teachers enact poetry and great literature, arithmetic teachers present lifelike math problems, etc.); using the arts and popular media to demonstrate our subjects.

2. *By being emotional about what we teach*—getting excited about new chapters, materials, and future events related to our subjects; showing wonder about discoveries and insights that emerge from studying our subjects; having feelings about the processes involved in our subject matter ("I feel frustrated by these problems myself." "I can't wait to begin the next unit." "I'm happy to discuss these topics with you.").

3. *By being interested in anything that relates to what we teach* —bringing in articles and newspaper clippings of current events that relate to what we teach; taking field trips; having credible guest speakers who work in areas related to our subject matter; leading study clubs; self-disclosing about our personal experiences related to the subject matter; sharing any new learning that we are experiencing as we pursue our subject.

4. *By being expert at what we teach*—knowing our field of study well and continuing to learn about it give testimony to its worth.

5. *By being a "fan" of what we teach*—devoting our time to understanding it better (joining related professional associations, going to topical conventions, etc.); following the leading scholars and journals in our field; rooting for greater awareness and appreciation of what we teach.

Strategy 3: *Associate the student with other students who are enthusiastic about the subject.* Enthusiasm is contagious. If the student has the opportunity to work with, be tutored by, or pursue a project or goal with students who are interested in and optimistic about the subject, she/he will have peers to model, and experience some group pressure to feel likewise. She/he will not be able to easily deny the value of the subject matter, and the resulting dissonance may lead to positive attitude change.

Strategy 4: *Positively confront the possible erroneous beliefs, expectations, and assumptions that may underlie the negative student attitude.*[8] Some students have mistaken beliefs that support their negative attitudes—e.g., "I could never do well in math"; "Social studies is always a drag"; "I won't get good grades in this subject." Assumptions of this sort lead to fear of and resistance toward a subject. In such cases, we might:

1. *Tactfully find out what the student may be telling herself/ himself that leads to the negative attitude.*

2. *If the student appears to have a self-defeating belief, point out as a teacher how negative feelings would naturally follow from such a belief*—i.e., "If you believe you're going to do poorly, you probably feel fearful and anxious about even trying to do some of the problems."

3. *Indicate other assumptions that might be more helpful to the student*—i.e., "You might try saying to yourself that this is a new class and a new teacher, and you have a chance to do better, or that this teacher is willing to help you and you can give it a try."

4. *Encourage the student to develop beliefs based on present reality that promote her/his well being*—i.e., "When you start to feel negative toward the subject, check out what you are telling yourself and see if it really helps you. Consider if there might be some other beliefs or expectancies that would do you more good. You might want to discuss this with me so I can give you feedback and other possible ways of looking at the issue that might be more helpful."

Strategy 5: *Make the first experience with the subject matter as positive as possible.* This approach is based on the idea that "first impressions are important." According to Scott, "Organization inhibits reorganization."[9] Therefore, the first time we experience anything that is new or occurs in a new and different setting, we are forming an impression that can have a lasting impact. This is a *critical period* in determining the ways we will respond to and feel about what we are experiencing. Since it is an initial experience, the student has not totally organized any beliefs and attitudes toward the subject and is more flexible and fluid, more open to change. The student's first impression will strongly influence how she/he accepts and receives future experiences with the subject matter. This essentially comes from the student's need for survival and predictability. The student who has a positive first experience will feel more safe and more willing to become involved in the subject matter at a later date. If not, the student will avoid the subject for reasons of self-protection. Everything we do to make that first lesson exciting, safe, and interesting will further open the door to more motivation to learn the related subject.

Attitude Toward the Self

"The greatest evil that can befall man is that he should come to think ill of himself."[10] Some students may not have a negative attitude toward us or the subject matter, but they may have a poor attitude toward themselves. This is often called "low self-esteem" or "bad self-concept." By any name, if this is true, it will probably significantly lower their motivation to learn. Combs and Rogers[11] have written that the maintenance and the enhancement of the perceived self are the motives behind all behavior. Combs describes the nature of motivation as "an insatiable need for the maintenance and enhancement of the self; not the physical self—but the phenomenal self of which the individual is aware, his self-concept."[12]

Each student strives to behave in ways that are consistent with her/his self-image. When the attitude toward the self with respect to learning is positive, the student develops a success-oriented personality which looks for ways to learn. When the attitude toward the self with respect to learning is negative, the student develops a failure-oriented personality which looks for ways to fail. In both instances, the student is attempting to be consistent with her/his self-image. Each step we take to help the student build a positive academic self-concept will reap benefits that should include a greater desire to learn.

Strategy 1: *Guarantee successful learning.* Seligman maintains that students with low academic self-concepts have learned to be helpless in school—to believe that nothing that they do will be right. He states, "Intelligence, no matter how high, cannot manifest itself if the child believes that his own actions will have no effect."[13] Concretely making certain that the student has a successful learning experience can alter such a mental set. Here are some guidelines:

1. *Segment instruction into units or increments that will definitely allow the student to progress in her/his learning* so that the student can say, "I know I learned something today."

2. *Give clear enough cues that allow the student to know where she/he is and where she/he is expected to go.* (Student perception—"I know where I am and where I'm going with this lesson.")

3. *Give the student immediate and specific feedback to learning responses.* (Student perception—"I always can find out how well I'm doing with this teacher.")

4. *Make sure the student knows the criteria by which learning will be evaluated.* (Student perception—"I know exactly what I can do to do well in this subject.")

Strategy 2: *Encourage the student.* Encouragement is any behavior on our part by which we show the student: (1) that we respect the student as a person, no matter what she/he learns; (2) that we trust and believe in the student's effort to learn; and (3) that the student can learn. Students need to be accepted as valued human beings without relationship to what they learn. For a student to realize that she/he is respected by the teacher only because of learning performance is dehumanizing. Such a criterion for teacher acceptance denies all the student's other worthy qualities, rejects her/his rights as a person, and makes the student into a "thing" that learns without feelings and dignity. As with any form of encouragement, the primary foundation is our caring and acceptance of the student. This forms the launching base for the ways we choose to show confidence and personal regard for their effort and learning. These include the following:

1. *Give recognition for real effort*—Any time a person attempts to learn something, she/he is taking a risk. Learning is a courageous act. Because students don't learn 100 percent of the time, some risk is always involved. We can help by acknowledging their effort and by making endeavor a valued personal trait. Any comment that says, "I like the way you try," can help the student see this effort as something to cherish in the process of learning.

2. *Show appreciation for student progress*—Any step in the direction of learning is an advancement. By demonstrating our awareness of this, we display feeling for its value and provide opportunity for the student to feel self-value.

3. *Minimize mistakes while the student is still struggling*—Sometimes learning is like a battle. The critical edge between advancement and withdrawal or between hope and despair is fragile at best. Reflection on a student's mistakes at such a critical moment is accentuated by the emotions at hand and is a sure way to encourage self-defeat.

4. *When learning is slow, divide the assignments into many short tasks*—This turns a single, long-distance accomplishment into many, more possible short-distance successes. This can give the student a greater feeling of progress, help the student maintain concentration, and enhance the student's academic confidence.

5. *For each task, demonstrate a confident and realistic expectancy for the student to learn*—Essentially this translates into the message, "You can do it," but without the implication that the task is easy or simple. Whenever we tell a student that something is easy, we have placed that student in a "lose–lose" dilemma. If she/he does the task, there is no reward because the task was easy in the first place, and if she/he fails, the feeling of despair is only heightened because the task was implied to be simple.

6. *Show faith in the student as a general learner*—This is an attitude toward the student. It reveals itself primarily in how we act toward the student. It is usually centered in our non-verbal communication. The tone of our voice, the look on our face, the way we stand, and our entire manner toward the student can display our confidence in her/him. Basically, the message should be, "No matter what, I will continue to believe in you and work with you." Whenever we give up on a student, we also give up on ourselves as teachers. By showing consistent trust in the student's capacity to learn, we help that student learn to trust herself/himself in transactions with us and in learning activities.

7. *Work with the student at the beginning of difficult tasks*—

Sometimes a student is afraid to attempt something new for fear of making a mistake or of failing. Just our proximity and minimal assistance can help the student to get involved and gain initial confidence to continue.

8. *Ask the student for help*—The implication behind any request for help is a sense of confidence that the helping person has assets and valued qualities.

9. *Emphasize learning from mistakes*—Students avoid things they're hit with. Mistakes can "club" students into negative self-concepts. Here we help the student to see a mistake as a way to improve future learning. Using mistakes to lower grades is like using water to drown a thirsty person.

10. *Reduce praise and increase encouragement*—Praise is usually given upon successful completion of a task. It emphasizes the product, not the process, of learning. For the insecure student, lack of praise can signify failure. It also means the student must wait until the end of learning in order to feel good about learning. Encouragement says the task itself is important and shows the intrinsic value of the act of learning.

Whenever we encourage students, we engage in essentially any behavior that strengthens the student's belief in herself/himself without damaging the student's relationship with others. It is not an act that requires extra money, new materials, or a changed curriculum. It does demand sensitivity and time. Those of us who have come to believe in ourselves have been encouraged—maybe by our parents, maybe by our teachers. But it was done. We come to value ourselves from those who value us.

Strategy 3: *Emphasize the student's personal causation*[14] *in her/ his learning.* A person who feels in control of her/his own fate and who assumes responsibility for her/his learning is a positively motivated, optimistic, and confident learner. A person who does not feel in control of her/his fate and who believes that someone else is the cause of her/his learning is a defensive, pessimistic, and insecure learner. In order for the student to feel that, "I can do it," when it comes to future learning, she/he must first be clearly aware that, "I did it," from previous experiences in learning.

In my opinion, this is the last piece of the puzzle. To guarantee successful learning and to encourage the student will have maximum motivational impact only if the student believes that she/he is personally responsible for learning. Some effective ways to ensure a sense of personal causation within the learner are:

1. *Allow the student to plan and set goals for learning*—A person who plans for something has a functional experience that validates that she/he is the originator and creator of that experience.

2. *Allow the student to make as many choices as possible about what, how, and when the student is to learn something*—Choice is the essence of responsibility: It permits the student to see that she/he is in charge of the learning experience.

3. *Allow the student to use self-evaluation procedures to check the progress of her/his learning*—When a student knows how to understand both the mistakes and the successes of her/his own learning, the student receives a concrete sense of her/his own participation in the learning act. Just as driving a car or riding a bike is a constant interplay of perception and feedback which accentuates our sense of control, self-evaluation procedures emphasize our control of learning experiences.

4. *Help the student to analyze her/his strengths and abilities in learning tasks*—e.g., "You seem to have a talent for explaining things well and probably could give a very interesting speech on how to . . . ." Knowing such assets gives each student a sense of the real power behind her/his learning and builds confidence.

5. *Have the student record or log her/his progress in learning tasks*—This concretely demonstrates to the student that growth and movement are taking place. It tangibly helps to refute discouragement and reduce pessimism.

6. *Help the student to analyze potential blocks to progress in learning*—This aids the student in preventing any sense of being overwhelmed by the subject matter and gives the student a chance to prepare for frustration and slower progress.

7. *When advisable, ask the student for a commitment to the learning task.* This gives the learner a sense of full participation. It prevents denial or withdrawal from personal responsibility for learning. When we ask a student, "Do you mean

it?" or, "Will you really try?" and we receive an affirmative answer, we are helping to amplify the student's sense of self-determination. However, this is not to be an overused or a frequent approach with the same student. If it becomes common or easily predictable, it will lack impact and emotional substance, becoming a mere game or manipulation.

Strategy 4: *Use group process methods to enhance a positive self-concept in the student.* Each student arrives at a sense of self through relationships with family, friends, fellow students, and teachers. The classroom peer group is a constant force that affects the student's self-appraisal, and these peers can be amazingly cruel, as well as magnificent sources of support and caring. There are many group activities that we can facilitate that give students the opportunity to show positive regard for and enjoyment of one another. In fact, there are at least a hundred, and Jack Canfield and Harold Wells have written a book aptly titled *100 Ways to Enhance Self Concept in the Classroom*—which is a great resource.[15]

Expectancy for Success

Sometimes students don't dislike their teachers, their subjects, or themselves. They just don't expect to do very well. They sit back and say, "On this, I'm really not going to be able to succeed." It is, in many instances, a very realistic outlook based on previous experience and self-awareness. Whenever students objectively do not expect to perform a task successfully, it is probably in their best interest not to get enthusiastic. If they do, they will only experience greater pain and disappointment if they fail. In fact, to try at something we don't believe we can do is not very intelligent behavior, and is often simply a waste of time.

This happens to students every day. They are given assignments or tests that they know they will not be able to do well on. On many occasions their teachers know this as well. In such situations students usually protect their psychological well being by remaining withdrawn or negative. Teachers often interpret this as apathy or rebellious behavior. It is really self-protection.

When we help a student to find a task that she/he wants to do and honestly expects to do successfully, motivation will not be a problem. But any time we give an assignment that the student cannot reasonably expect to do well on, we will probably have a motivational problem to contend with. In such instances, we can demonstrate clearly that the learning task is concretely possible for the student to achieve.

Strategy 1: *Interview the student.* When a student does not expect to succeed, it is important to understand *from the student's point of view* what is it that she/he thinks will prevent her/his learning. Such an interview should contain questions that are initiated with the words "what" and "how"—i.e., "What is it that you consider to be difficult?" or, "How do you think some problems might arise?" Avoid using questions beginning with "why." These can lead to a defensive posture, can increase an excuse mentality, and tend to avoid the student's feelings.

The advantage of the strategy is that what may be obvious to the student may not be obvious to us. I am reminded of the wonderful story of Princess Minnie Moons by James Thurber. When the king found out his daughter wanted the moon, he thought it was an impossible wish and became frustrated and hopeless. As a last resort he asked her what she considered the moon to be. The princess told him it resembled a small gold coin. With this information he was able to grant her wish. Teaching isn't a fairy tale, but until we know what the student's sense of expectancy is, we are guessing at best and may be missing the best ways to help each one along.

Strategy 2: *Use goal-setting methods.* The advantage of this method is that it brings the future into the present and allows the student to become aware of what it is necessary to do in order to have a successful learning experience. Not only does it prevent the student "from getting in over her/his head" but also it gives the student a chance to specifically evaluate and plan for those obstacles that prevent achievement. With the goal-setting model, the student knows that she/he is in command and can calculate what to do to avoid wasting time or experiencing self-defeat. Thus, before even beginning the learning task, the student knows that her/his effort will be worthwhile and has an actual sense that there is a good probability for success.

There are many different methods of goal setting. The one that follows is an eclectic adaptation from various models in the literature.

If the learning experience is to be initiated, the following criteria are to be met as well as planned with the student:

1. *Achievability*
   a. Is there enough time to reach the goal? If not, can more time be found, or should the goal be divided into smaller goals?
   b. Can the student do it with the skills and knowledge at hand? If not, is there any assistance available, and how *dependable* is that assistance?

2. *Believability*—What is the level of the student's self-confidence for the goal? Are we sure we are not cajoling or manipulating the student into something? Does the student at least think she/he has a reasonable chance of doing it?

3. *Measurability*—How will the student specifically be able to gauge her/his progress or achievement? This can be something as simple as problems completed, pages read, exercises finished, etc. The main thing is that a way of measuring is decided upon so that feedback is a tangible reality for self-evaluation.

4. *Desirability*—Is the goal something the student *wants* to do? She/he may *have* to do it or *should* do it, but is it wanted as well? If it isn't, then the satisfaction level and sense of personal responsibility for the student will be far less. Goal setting can be used for *must* situations, but this is best handled if we are open about it and admit to the student the reality of the situation to avoid any sense of manipulation or game playing.

5. *Focusing*—Some plan by which the goal is daily placed in the student's awareness is important to avoid forgetting or procrastination. Repression, denial, and the attractiveness of other realities are powerful barriers to progress. Effective reminders such as outlines, chalkboard messages, daily logs, etc., help to reduce their potential and aid us to refrain from unnecessary dependencies and nagging.

6. *Motivating*—Is the process of reaching the learning goal somehow stimulating, competence building, reinforcing, affectively positive, or need gratifying? This is necessary to maintain perseverance because initial motivation may wear thin.

7. *Commitment*—Is the goal so valued that the student can make a formal or informal gesture to pledge her/his effort and responsibility? This can be anything from a statement such as, "I'm really going to try," to a handshake to a contract. This affirms the student's self-awareness of her/his involvement and allows for the development of self-esteem.

If the above criteria are not met, the learning goal is probably in need of alteration or abandonment. If the criteria have been met, there is an excellent probability that the goal can be achieved. At least three more things can then be done.

8. *Identify resources within and outside of the student*—The student benefits from knowing her/his own power. Very little is accomplished through luck. Her/his ability to write, speak, spell, etc., is to be accentuated to indicate what can be utilized with confidence. All people at times question or doubt their talents. Our affirmation of these talents helps students to sustain and build their capacities. To identify resources outside of the student such as tutors, libraries, materials, etc., helps the student to more easily reach out and appreciate the interdependence of learning.

9. *Preplan to consider and remove potential obstacles to learning*—The question for the student is, "What do you think might interfere with the achievement of your goal?" This may include television watching, extracurricular activities, certain peers, or even lack of a quiet place to study. To plan ahead for the reduction of these inhibitors will decrease their obstructive power and give the student added strength to contend with them.

10. *Arrange a goal review schedule*—A small amount of time to check progress will give us and the student a chance to evaluate and regain momentum. Minor distraction and interferences can be more easily eliminated. Time sequencing and refinement of planning will help to encourage the student. Above all, if progress has deteriorated, don't ask "why" but re-examine the criteria. A question such as, "What did you do instead?" may help to uncover hidden distractors or competing goals.

Repeated use of goal-setting methods not only has a good probability of substantially increasing the student's expectancy for success but also documents for the student that she/he can shape and direct her/his own life.

Strategy 3: *Use contracting methods.* In many learning situations the curriculum is predetermined. The society and/or the school system mandates that students must learn to multiply, compose sentences, be aware of certain historical facts, etc. In such circumstances a contract (which is really a short form of goal setting) may be used as an agreement between the student and the teacher that specifies the exact ways to achieve and demonstrate a learning goal. Because contracts, with student agreement, detail what is to be done and how it is to be accomplished, there is far less chance of the ambiguity that leads to student anxiety, frustration, and fear of failure.

Such a contract, based on our diagnosis of the student's academic strengths, weaknesses, and learning style, contains:

1. What the student will learn.

2. How the student can demonstrate that she/he has learned the specified information, applications, skills, etc.

3. The degree of proficiency expected of the student.

4. The choice of resource and activity alternatives for learning.

For example: Date _____

1. Within the next two weeks I will learn to correctly multiply single-digit numbers ranging between 5 and 9—e.g., 5×6, $6 \times 7, 7 \times 8, 8 \times 9, 9 \times 5$.

2. When I feel prepared, I will ask to take a mastery test containing 50 problems from this range of multiplication facts.

3. I will complete this contract when I can finish the mastery test with no more than three errors.

4. My preparation and study will involve choosing work from the workbook activities, number games, and filmstrip materials.

Signed,

Student _____

There are many different contracting procedures.[16] While the one we choose may be based on personal preference, the two overriding guidelines must remain student agreement and clarity in order to avoid expectancy of failure and to ensure student responsibility for learning.

Strategy 4: *Use programmed materials.* Although programmed materials have not been found to be an innovation superior to other means of learning, for the student with a low expectancy for success they may be a valuable resource. Because they are usually sequenced with steps small enough to guarantee progress through the ample use of cues and because they prompt with immediate feedback, a student with low confidence for learning a particular subject may feel reassured by this type of structure. Just as a detailed and clearly illustrated map can guide a stranger through foreign territory, programmed materials can help to build confidence for the student through what might appear to be an alien and exotic subject.

Programmed materials vary widely in quality and creative design. However, as professionals, we must know their availability in our subject matter and use them where appropriate.

We have discussed many ways to facilitate motivation relative to attitude. There is no one best way, but there are numerous intelligent alternatives. Which we choose will be most helpful when selected on the basis of our sensitive awareness of ourselves, our students, and our situation. Each time we present ourselves to students, we are dealing with human beings under the influence of their attitudes. Everything we can do to help that impinging force to be positive will be not only to their advantage but to ours as well. The tragedies of teaching emanate from a lack of awareness. Because attitudes are often hidden within the students in any classroom, we must probe to know their depth and to free their motivational force.

Chapter 3

Needs:
The Energy
Behind Behavior

A *need* is a condition experienced by the individual as a force that leads the person to move in the direction of a goal. The achievement of the goal is capable of releasing or ending the feeling of the need or its related tension. Hunger (a need) leads to a search for food (a goal). When enough food is eaten, the need or tension of hunger is ended. All people live with an unending sense of need. Not to feel any sense of need is tantamount to ending our existence. Some needs are unlearned (thirst), and some are learned (the need to achieve). What type of need we are currently experiencing is based on our history of learning, the current situation, and the last need that was fulfilled.

Needs motivate learning, especially at the beginning of any academic task. One way to view successful teaching is as a process that meets the fundamental needs of students. When students do not want to learn, it is quite probable either that they are experiencing needs that interfere with the learning process or that our teaching neglects, satiates, or threatens their current need state. Take, for instance, a student who refuses to do a geography assignment that is achievable, challenging, and stimulating. The student may not want to do it because: (1) she/he is worried about failing a math test and wants. to prepare for it (safety need); (2) she/he is concerned about an argument with a friend (love need); or (3) she/he simply has to use the bathroom and feels bodily distress (physical need). Undoubtedly, there are many more possibilities. The critical realization for us is that students do not "instinctively" want to hassle teachers. According to need theory, they simply take the shortest route to goals that are based on their felt needs. When students do not want to start to learn or when they want to stop continuing to learn, a basic question for us is, "What fundamental need is now influencing the student?" Answers to this question will help us to know what to do to facilitate motivation.

There are many different theories relative to the concept of need. In fact, they can create confusion because any time we see a student trying to achieve a goal, we can explain her/his behavior by inferring a need for the goal—e.g., for ice cream, for a book, for attention, for a new toy. Among the many, I have chosen Maslow's[1] need theory as the basic structure of this chapter and as the foundation for the need factor in the model. His is the most holistic and dynamic, offering an interrelated set of guidelines to enhance student motivation.

Maslow believed that need gratification was the most important single principle underlying all human development. He proposed a hierarchy of needs arranged in order of prepotency. This means that when needs are satisfied at one level, the next higher order of needs becomes predominant in influencing behavior. Unless a lower need is at least partially fulfilled, it is difficult for the next higher need to be influential on the person's behavior. These needs, from lowest to highest, are found in Figure 6.

Figure 6

Highest	SELF-ACTUALIZATION NEEDS	(G)
↑	ESTEEM NEEDS	(D)
	LOVE NEEDS	(D)
	SAFETY NEEDS	(D)
Lowest	PHYSIOLOGICAL NEEDS	(D)

In this sense, a student who is slightly sleepy (physical need) could probably study for a test (safety and/or self-esteem need). But a student who has not slept in three days would care little about studying.

It is important to note that the lower four needs are deficiency needs (D) while self-actualization is a growth need (G). These needs differ in the following ways:

1. People act to *get rid* of deficiency needs and satisfy them to *avoid* problems. Their consummation leads to a sense of relief and/or satiation. The satisfaction of growth needs *produces health* and leads to *pleasure* and a desire for *further fulfillment*. This is the difference between passing a test (deficiency need) and creating an original poem (growth need).

2. Deficit needs tend to be *selfishly centered* and *dependent on others* for fulfillment. Growth needs tend to be *self-directed* with *empathetic regard for others* and based on *personal standards*. Compare a spoiled student who whines for attention with a responsible student who seeks personal goals for self-improvement.

3. Learning from deficit needs tends to be *extrinsically rewarding* while learning from growth needs tends to be *intrinsically rewarding*. In the former, the student is dependent on teacher approval, grades, test scores, etc., for a sense of satisfaction. In the latter, the process of learning and the act of doing it provide the student with satisfaction.

I am talking in extremes now, and I think it wise to say that most behavior is to some degree a combination of deficit motivation and some degree of growth motivation. As teachers, we can help to increase growth motivation by making the process of learning as free as possible from deficit motivation by the way we present our subject matter and organize the conditions for learning it. Maslow insightfully instructs us when he states, "Furthermore, if we clearly and fully recognize that these noble and good impulses come into existence and grow potent primarily as a consequence of the prior gratification of the more demanding animal needs, we should certainly speak less exclusively of self-control, inhibition, discipline, etc. and more frequently of spontaneity, gratification, and self-choice."[2]

I am convinced that most of us would like to give freedom of choice to our students whenever we teach. Yet I know that in the back of our minds when we look at our students, we expect some to make good choices that are self-directed and personally productive, while for others we fear that the choices will be self-destructive and wasteful. It is this dilemma that leads to our conflict and anxiety. Maslow also was aware of this, and his words are worth considering:

61

Why is it so hard and painful for some to grow forward? Here we must become more fully aware of the fixative and regressive power of ungratified deficiency needs, of the attractions of safety and security, of the functions of defense and protection against pain, fear, loss and threat, of the need for courage in order to grow ahead.

Every human being has *both* sets of forces within him. One set clings to safety and defensiveness out of fear, tending to regress backward, hanging on to the past, *afraid* to grow . . . , *afraid* to take chances, *afraid* to jeopardize what he already has, *afraid* of independence, freedom and separateness. The other set of forces impels him forward toward wholeness of self and uniqueness of self, toward full functioning of all his capacities, toward confidence in the face of the external world at the same time that he can accept his deepest, real, unconscious self.[3]

Then what do we do? That is the real question. Maslow did not leave us hanging. His advice?

In this process, the environment (parents, therapists, teachers) is important in various ways, even though the ultimate choice must be made by the child:

A. It can gratify his basic needs for safety, belongingness, love and respect, so that he can feel unthreatened, autonomous, interested and spontaneous and thus dare to choose the unknown.

B. It can help by making the growth choice positively attractive and less dangerous, and by making the regressive choice less attractive and more costly.[4]

Maslow's own diagram in Figure 7[5] illustrates this approach.

Figure 7

---

*ENHANCE
THE DANGERS*   *ENHANCE THE
ATTRACTIONS*

Safety ◄———— < PERSON > ————► *Growth*

*MINIMIZE THE
ATTRACTIONS*   *MINIMIZE THE
DANGERS*

That is our goal—when we arrange learning opportunities, we can attempt to increase the safety and attractiveness of those choices that allow student growth as well as to decrease the safety and attractiveness of those choices that prohibit student growth. Some ideas on how to do this are contained in the pages that follow.

Two types of strategies will be outlined for the subfactors under need. One type of strategy deals with how the content of the subject matter presented relates to a specific need. The second type deals with the process of learning itself and with how the presentation and approach to learning, as facilitated by the teacher, enhance motivation with respect to a specific need.

Physiological Needs

Unless the basic physiological needs are met, learning becomes a difficult, if not impossible, task because the student's energy is devoted to coping with the pain and state of deprivation her/his body is feeling. These basic needs are usually for food, water, air, rest, activity, sex, and sensory satisfaction. This is why properly timed recess breaks, adequate provision for bathroom needs, and even the availability of a water fountain can make or break any well-planned learning activity.

Sleepy students are crabby and cranky students. Because their blood sugar is low, hungry students are often restless and hostile students. Students who are too hot or too cold usually have just one thing on their minds and that's the temperature in the room. Very little motivation for learning is going to take place under any of these circumstances. These needs are so obviously within the basic rights of the students that I don't believe special strategies should be outlined for them. Humane consideration and whatever means are available are to be used to satisfy them or we can forget about teaching. These needs must be met before any concern for learning can be expected on the part of the student.

However, some physiological needs are not so patently obvious. One of the most easily missed and most often abused is the need for sensory satisfaction or, as it is more commonly known, the need for stimulation. This is a pervasive need which constantly influences student motivation. My respect for it is of such magnitude that it is a major factor in the motivation model and will have the next chapter devoted to its understanding and application. Right now, we will

agitated state, I could only deduce that this person was insensitive to our needs.

Safety Needs

These needs deal with the basic security of the individual. They are arrived at through a sense of stability and freedom from fear and anxiety. They are partly made up of the needs for structure, order, and reasonable limits. Students as well as teachers want a safe, orderly, predictable, lawful, and organized classroom where the dangerous and chaotic do not occur.

Students appreciate and prefer a regular and orderly learning environment where consistently fair discipline allows for safe limits for their behavior. If they are threatened by fellow students and/or teachers, there will be little motivation for learning but there will be high motivation to escape the threat. It is important to note that many tests have been passed and assignments completed, not out of a motivation to learn, but out of a desire to avoid punishment. *This is coercion or negative motivation.* At best, it results in learning-directed behavior of the shortest duration with future avoidance of the subject matter. Its long-term effects are a repulsion for school and learning in general.

Students can be frightened into doing academic tasks—but probably less so than 20 years ago. We can lower their grades, fail them, and take away their privileges in order to get them to study and produce. But each year it gets more difficult to scare them at younger and younger ages. We know this and wonder why. "Why can't we *make* them learn?" Some say it is because students today are more disrespectful of authority or spoiled because parents are too permissive and the culture is disintegrating. Maybe—but I don't think so. I think there are more than a few reasons, but I'll offer my top three. First, I agree with Glasser and his concept of the *identity society*[6] where many young people today have been reared in relative affluence and come to school with greater self-esteem needs. Most of their safety needs have been met at home, and we just can't scare them into thinking that if they don't learn, life is going to be unbearable and their futures ruined. Their daily life does not phenomenologically support such impending threat. Secondly, they are much more aware through television, their parents, and other media that they have a right to be treated with decency and not constantly threatened. They just won't take the abuse as easily as we did. And thirdly, their parents have been through the fear system of education and don't support it. Few parents tell their child to do "anything the teacher says." They have, and they know it hasn't helped. As teachers, we have lost the mythology of being virtuous, expert, and infallible. In light of this, it is self-defeating to follow coercive tactics with students. We need to guarantee our own safety by finding other ways to enhance student motivation.

With students being less apparently frightened into learning, we may be seduced into thinking that they are less anxious. I doubt it. Unfortunately, one of the things we lose with our innocence is our willingness to expose our fears. When an infant is frightened, she/he does not hesitate to display her/his apprehension. As we grow older, we increase our inhibition to show that we are frightened. Being mature and adult also means being better able to disguise our reactions of dread and dismay. As students grow older, they are less likely to show their vulnerability. They may go through long periods of anxiety before they indicate their disapproval. They may be disobedient, be uncooperative, and do poorly in learning with feelings of anxiety that are imperceptible to us. We only know that they didn't do the work or are not learning. Because of our own frustration, we can easily remain insensitive to how they feel. We may not be able to make them study, but we may be able to make them suffer. Our sensitivity and willingness to abandon coercive tactics can effectively help to reduce such feelings.

Strategy 1: *When relevant, select content, examples, and projects that relate to the safety needs of the students.* One of the main goals of education is to use knowledge to neutralize fear. We are less frightened of lightning because we know something about it. Students at every age level are naturally interested in learning about things that can reduce their everyday fears. For young children this often has to do with such elements as thunder, fire, storms, the dark, etc. Every good storyteller knows this and uses these ingredients to spice the tales she/he narrates. Young children love spooky stories because they verge on the unknown that needs to be known.

With older students, peer relations, travel, securing independence, getting a job and vocational interests, and family relations are subjects that naturally appeal to their desire for greater security. The main thing is to find those areas of concern specific to students' safety needs and to employ them as an enhancement to what is being taught from math to mysticism. A guide in this area might be to simply ask students in an informal manner what worries them. Then use this information to enhance the subject matter at hand or to create the foundation for projects and assignments.

Strategy 2: *Reduce or remove components of the learning environment that lead to failure or fear.* Most of these suggestions have been covered under the subfactor of "Attitude Toward the Subject and Learning Situation" which was discussed in the previous chapter. However, I would like to emphasize a few of these strategies and add some new ones.

1. *Avoid creating any learning situation that leads a student to a sense of failure.* I strongly agree with Glasser that student failure serves no positive purpose.[7] It may tell her/him what she/he can't do or allow for a comparison with other students, but its side effects of negative self-concept, anxiety, and lowered motivation far outweigh any sense of benefit. This doesn't mean that students shouldn't experience mistakes, limited achievement, or even lack of completion, but it does mean they can learn from their mistakes, find out what they need to learn, and continue to progress if so desired. Our verbal or nonverbal message to the student is, "No matter how well you do, I will help you to learn. I will not give up on you. You can't fail. You can only stop trying." Failure is phenomenological. We only fail when we accept this position ourselves. We can stop doing things that we are unsuccessful at when we have other needs or goals. Whether that is failure or good judgment is in the eyes of the doer. Our goal is to encourage intelligent choices based on reasonable judgment by our students.

2. *For skills and convergent learning processes (known and agreed-upon information or knowledge), use a mastery approach.* Mastery learning considers individual student differences in learning rates and assumes that most students can master at least a minimum level of learning if given enough time. Tests are used to diagnose and instruct, not to discriminate. Competitiveness and normal curve grading procedures are eliminated. The principle is that students are better off if they are taught less, but thoroughly learn what they *are* taught.[8]

3. *Make sure the student understands the academic expectancies and criteria for evaluation on any test or unit of learning.* For most of us, the first day of any college course brought an inquiry about, "What do I have to do and how do I have to do it in order to pass this class?" When we received clear answers, we were relieved or more anxious, but when we received inadequate or ambiguous responses, we were definitely more anxious. This is just as true for third graders. The safety needs of all students demand clear expectancies to feel secure about learning.

4. *Act to remove or eliminate any aspects of cultural, sexual or racial discrimination.* In this respect, we must be sensitive to our students, our materials, and most especially ourselves.

a. Do we accept and respect *all* students in our classes?

b. Do we have fair standards and expectancies for *all* students?

c. How aware are we of our own prejudices? How do they affect us?

With integration and cultural pluralism, our schools are the living environment for social change. As teachers, we can model attitudes and behaviors that enhance relations in our classes by showing acceptance and fairness to all groups of students, or we can perpetuate institutional racism which denies the basic safety needs of minority students. I do not know how to briefly provide the best guidelines for this endeavor, but I suggest the book *Multicultural Nonsexist Education*[9] as an excellent reference.

5. *Use a discipline approach that is fair, student accepted, well understood, and consistently applied.* There are many different philosophies and theories of discipline. Gordon, Glasser, Dreikurs, Dinkmeyer, and Krumboltz have produced comprehensive models to follow. The central idea is to safeguard the learning process so that students can live and learn in an atmosphere that is secure and relaxed. We are the persons legally responsible for facilitating that atmosphere, and whichever theory or combination of theories we apply will depend on our values, students, and situation. Probably the single most important criterion here is consistency. When students cannot have some assurance that we maintain a regular and harmonious approach to disruption and problems, their world becomes constantly unpredictable and chaotic—no longer safe to learn in.

Strategy 3: *Create a learning environment that is organized and orderly.* One of the easiest ways to make a person psychotic is to make that person dependent on someone and then to have that someone treat the person in a totally unpredictable manner. Students need a sense of routine and orderliness in their daily living. This reduces stress and provides the energy necessary to make choices for leading a responsible life. However, we must proceed cautiously because routines can become ruts and the need for safety a compulsion that avoids positive learning and growth. What is advocated here is that each classroom should have a regular procedure by which materials are received and shared, by which students know how to cooperate, by which grievances are aired, and by which basic order is maintained and each student's rights upheld. This does not mean that learning should not be imaginative, exciting, or sometimes even unpredictable. The routines and organization provide the foundation from which the student can mentally, emotionally, and physically leap into the process of learning, just as the floor provides the foundation for every dancer's step and graceful creation of motion.

Strategy 4: *Don't expect initiative and self-discipline from insecure students.* As a student I have always been amazed by instructors who on the first day of class asked, "Well, what do you want to learn about (new subject)?" This question was usually greeted by throat clearing, shuffling feet, and anxious silence. Who knows what to ask for on the first day of class? First of all, trust isn't yet established between the teacher and the students so very few are willing to be vulnerable and take the risk of making a request. Secondly, the teacher is seen as the expert and most students want some guidance. And thirdly, most students aren't familiar enough with the subject to know what to ask for. I won't belabor the point except to say that the basis for insecurity is not knowing when or how to act around a given topic or situation. Initiative and self-discipline at any age level emanate from self-confidence. Teacher expectancies for these assets only put insecure students in a double bind that more severely threatens their safety needs. (This is one of the most dominant errors I have witnessed in new and well-intentioned teachers.)

Strategy 5: *Introduce the unfamiliar through the familiar.* If you're starting a new topic, connect it to the last topic studied. If you're beginning a new skill, compare it to a skill already learned by your students. If you're trying a more complex lesson, demonstrate how it relates to a more simple one. This makes the students feel safer, more confident, and, therefore, more willing to risk learning. Whenever people anticipate new experiences, they usually ask "like" questions: "What does it taste like?" "Who does he look like?" "What does it feel like?" This helps the person to assimilate the potential experience with the known past and to feel more secure about attempting it. The same is true for building initiative in novel learning situations.

Belongingness and Love Needs

These needs make up the person's innate desire for affectionate relationships and for a place in the group with an accepted identity. For students this means that they can feel respected and a part of the class, giving and receiving genuine affection among their fellow students and teachers.

Loneliness, alienation, rejection, and rootlessness are the feelings of students whose belongingness needs are unsatisfied. We all crave a sense of territory—someplace we can go and be ourselves and be accepted for ourselves. Students want friends in school and something to join and form their sense of self from. To me, school spirit is a primal herding instinct, and school teams and activities are the functional symbols around which we flock and relate.

The need for affection is probably stronger today among our students than in previous years. Due to our mobility, breakdown of traditional groupings, scatter of extended families, and steady urbanization, our young people come to school with more of these unmet needs than ever before. The strong and pervasive adolescent subculture is only one symptom of the trend. It is a reality of our times to which we as teachers must respond.

Schools have been established as places of learning. Both formally and informally this usually means cognitive learning—reading, writing, and arithmetic. The socialization of students and its related ties to friendship and a sense of belonging are generally seen as secondary goals. Our primary grades often stress the love aspect of education, but as the student grows older, we say that we have to "get down to business" and begin a continual evolution toward competitiveness, specialization of subject matter, and emphasis on grade point averages. To some extent this is related to the basic safety needs of graduation,

71

job security, and college entry. I can understand this and accept its powerful appeal to parents and social leaders. However, while students are learning, they cannot constantly relate to these future-oriented needs. They require a continuing sense of identity and kinship among their peers. The research on dropouts strongly supports this view.[10]

I have come to have such respect for this position that I consider affect (emotional climate) as a major motivational factor during learning and will discuss it at length in a future chapter. Presently we will deal with the need for belonging on a more individual basis as it relates to motivation.

Strategy 1: *When relevant, select content, examples, and projects that relate to the belongingness and love needs of the students.*

1. *Whenever possible, use examples with which your students can identify.* Instead of "Dick and Jane" or "two boys" or "a woman" or "some adults" or "group of teachers" as characters in a figurative example, use names of students from your class, or place characters in the same grade or age level as your students, or offer relatives such as parents, uncles, aunts, and cousins, as well as familiar teachers, to illustrate instances of behavior for the subject taught.

2. *Use the familiar*—local neighborhoods, resident cities and states, recent movies, television programs, and media presentations, as well as popular sports figures and rock and movie stars—*to vitalize projects, case studies, and sample situations relative or analogous to subject matter.*

3. *Make sure that the books, materials, and examples employed in class positively represent the ethnic and racial composition of the students.* When relevant, invite local personalities who represent such groups to talk and work with the class.

4. *Gain a sense of the socialization preferences of your students.* Use examples of friendship, kinship, family, romance, dating behavior, loyalty, and commitment to accentuate topics, examples, and themes in any subject matter. *Charlotte's Web* has done it for children, *Catcher in the Rye* for adolescents, and *Love Story* for college students.

In all of the above suggestions, the main idea is to constantly ask ourselves, "Is what I am offering my students something they can identify with?" If the answer is Yes, *from the students' perception,* motivation and involvement will be difficult for them to resist.

Strategy 2: *Increase or create components in the learning environment that tell the student that she/he is wanted and that significant others care about her/him.*

1. *Learn and use the names of your students as quickly as possible.* We all enjoy being called by our names. It is probably the quickest and most instantaneous form of recognition. My personal goal in this respect is to learn all my students' names within one week. (I actually have to study to do this, but the satisfaction of my students and the payoff for initiating good relations are immense.) It is just as important for students to learn each other's names as fast as possible. Name cards or mixer games can be used for this purpose. These strategies are found in most human relations and communications textbooks.

2. *Interview each student personally.* This will help you to better understand her/his goals, needs, personal lifestyles, and family situations, as well as hobbies and interests. Consider the benefits of such a discussion:

   a. Each student will have a face-to-face contact with you in which she/he can relate beyond academics.

   b. Each student will know that you know her/him better as a person, and will also have a sense of you as an individual.

   c. This interview will affirm your caring and involvement with each student.

   d. You will probably give each student an experience that she/he has had with few teachers. This is often enough to stimulate a sense of reciprocal commitment.

It is important to remember that the interview should be light and not an interrogation or prying into personal matters. If you can't find the time, construct a personal data questionnaire, and use it to understand and share information that enhances the social atmosphere of your class.

3. *Keep 5 × 7 cards for each student.* Record "highlights" of her/his academic achievements, personal satisfactions, goals accomplished, etc., and specifically refer to these points in conversation and

working relationships with students to concretely "accentuate the positive" and build morale in times of stress and difficulty.

4. *Celebrate student birthdays, send get-well cards, bring spontaneous treats, and do the "little" things that show you care.* To some of us this may seem trite, but I believe that no single act or few significant behaviors give students a sense of affection. Rather it is an accumulation of small kindnesses, minute acknowledgments, and touches of warmth that tell students that they belong and are wanted.

Strategy 3: *Designate classroom duties and responsibilities in such a way that each student becomes a functioning member of the group.* With student consultation, rotate roles of leadership, tasks of assistance, committee work, and privileges to give everyone a chance. This becomes a dynamic system by which every pupil can feel and act out her/his role. A class is analogous to a family in which every member has rights, responsibilities, and privileges. Unless these are totally shared, someone can become a minority, withdrawn and forgotten. It also provides for the giving and receiving elements necessary to a healthy group.

Most yearbooks are a striking indictment against the social processes of high school. A few people dominate the pictures, appearing in most of the club, team, and council pictures, with the rest of the students part of the faceless masses in group composition for each grade level. We defend this by saying that most kids are "followers." Yet, the system we design can allow for more participation, especially at the classroom level. Our responsibility is to create an environment of participation—to make it difficult to be left out. (I will treat this more comprehensively when discussing the group dynamic in Chapter 5. Also refer to "Attitude Toward the Teacher" in Chapter 2 for more strategies to enhance each student's sense of belonging.)

Esteem Needs

According to Maslow, esteem needs may be divided into two types. The first group emphasizes self-respect and the inner desire for strength, achievement, adequacy, mastery, competence, confidence in the face of the world, independence, and freedom. These needs are self-reliant and based usually on personal standards and values. The second group of esteem needs are more other-directed and related to esteem from other people. These are prestige, status, fame, glory, dominance, recognition, attention, importance, dignity, and appreciation. Maslow has cautioned that this set of esteem needs, although very powerful, is more dangerous; these needs can lead to severe dependency on others, make the self more prone to manipulation, and encourage an unpredictable and false sense of self, as well as distort and impede acceptance of the self. He sees the most healthy self-esteem as based on deserved respect from others which comes as a result of our real capacity, competence, and adequacy for the task. For students this means that their motivation will be facilitated by helping them to gain a realistic awareness of their strengths and by allowing them to responsibly achieve and develop an honest sense of personal effectiveness and reasonable independence.

Students will no doubt continue to be motivated from a desire to gain status, attention, fame, and approval. We would be unwise to deny or dismiss such aspirations. How these needs are encouraged and what relative importance they have to those of self-respect are the crucial considerations we must make in influencing student motivation. My suggestion is to relegate the other-directed esteem needs to a secondary role and to make students aware, by our own teaching and modeling, of the seductiveness and limited potential for self-growth that these needs foster.

Because I regard the need for competence as crucial to student motivation in any learning situation, I have placed it as a major motivational factor in the model. The relationship of competence (as well as achievement motivation) as a process in teaching behavior will be fully discussed in Chapter 6. For now, I will treat this and the other self-esteem needs as factors related to the content and introduction of subject matter.

Strategy 1: *Offer the opportunity for responsible attainment of learning goals that affirm the student's identity or role.* Under the need for belonging, we stressed the importance of strategies that accepted the student's identity. Now we want to encourage strategies that allow the student to enhance her/his identity through responsible learning. This is the meaning of that educational jargon constantly thrown at teachers under the cloak of "relevance." Relevant subject matter is anything we ask students to learn that helps them to achieve goals that support their identity. If I see myself as a future car mechanic or athlete and if I am asked to study engine maintenance or the relationship of running to physics, I am receiving a relevant curriculum. I am studying about something that is important to the goals my identity offers for me.

In presenting any subject matter to students, a guiding question is, "What do my students see themselves as, and how can I offer this in such a way as to relate to or enhance that identity?" Another equally important question is, "How can my students' learning of this make them more effective at what they are or what they want to be?" That is why *you* are reading this book. You don't want to be just a teacher. You want to be an *effective* teacher.

Strategy 2: *Offer students subject matter, assignments, and learning modes that appeal to and complement their strengths and assets.* We don't learn with luck. We learn by employing skills, knowledge, and experience gained from previous learning to new learning. It is much better to flow than to push. On a day-to-day basis our goal is more likely to be to make the "leap of learning" into a small step. In order to do this, we have to know our students' capabilities. They need to know them, too. When introducing and initiating a learning activity, some discussion with the student as to how this experience will build on and be related to her/his current abilities should enhance immediate involvement.

Strategy 3: *Offer students subject matter in such a way that it enhances the student's independence as a learner and as a person.* Essentially, this means providing subject matter that allows the student to realize greater self-sufficiency and self-determination. When students can learn to live, and realize that they are learning to live, a most exciting event has occurred. Reading literally opens the door to every library in the nation. Math helps us to buy groceries, keep a savings account, and budget our money for the things we want. Understanding a map makes travel more possible. Learning is for owning our lives, for being able to depend on ourselves, for making us what we want to be. Every time we show students, "even in the smallest fashion," how this is possible, we appeal to their basic need for independence. In fact, if we cannot see how our subject matter can do this, it is time to reconsider its value.

Strategy 4: *Plan activities to allow students to publicly display and share their talents and work.* No doubt the attention, recognition, and appreciation of fellow students and others will enhance motivation and effort. However, the emphasis need not be on competition, comparative evaluation, or awards which stress winning for student performance. Rather, the emphasis might be on sharing, gaining feedback, investigating, appreciating uniqueness of style, and understanding personal differences. Every serious artist wants her/his work published or publicly displayed for many reasons. Recognition is certainly a part of this motivation, but so is the sharing of insight—the awareness that public acceptance affirms and gives credit to the talent and beauty of the artistic endeavor and that the feedback and criticism that result allow for further evolution of the person's growth as an artist.

Students have similar esteem needs and can meet them by having their work available to other students, parents, and faculty through:

1. Oral presentations.

2. Public displays on tables, walls, and bulletin boards.

3. Chalkboard demonstrations.

4. Discussion processes.

5. Role playing.

6. Fishbowl techniques (a small group of students works or relates among themselves, while the rest of the group is circled around them and observes them).

7. Collected publication of students' work in a school or "classroom" book, newspaper, or magazine.

8. Photograph collections of student activities, field trips, or projects.

9. Films, slide presentations, and audio or audiovisual taping of student performances.

10. Open-house activities that invite community participation and observation.

Again, the emphasis for all of these suggestions is on deserved respect which comes from the appreciation of others for what students do—and not the manipulation of competitive structures or a contest-like atmosphere.

The Need for Self-Actualization

These needs are found in a person's desire for self-fulfillment. They are the internal strivings within each person for those activities that allow the individual to experience her/his potential and to be what she/he is—or is capable of becoming. These growth needs are most readily met by learning that is intrinsically rewarding (the doing of the activity is in itself satisfying). For children this emerges at its earliest stages with behavior based on curiosity, exploration, and creativity.

Even though the previously discussed deficiency needs are to be met before these growth needs can fully emerge, the need for self-actualization is often present on a partial basis. Physically well, safe, accepted, and respected students at any age will show their need to explore and create. The goal is to establish, as often as possible, those conditions within the classroom to maximize and enhance the learning choices based on growth needs. When such an atmosphere exists, we can make learning attractive; we can minimize the danger around learning, which is intrinsically rewarding and invested in the self-actualization of our students.

"Learning for the sake of learning" is an old cliché which as a goal for teachers may seem too idealistic with today's students. Yet, it is the fundamental principle behind intrinsic motivation and self-actualization. That it is rare does not mean that it is impossible. It is a basic purpose of education for which what we do has meaning. Without it, teaching is merely training—no longer an art or a profession.

And now the practical.

Strategy 1: *Provide students with the opportunity to select topics, projects, and assignments that appeal to their curiosity, sense of wonder, and need to explore.* The way to begin is to ask ourselves what it is about the subject matter that we teach that still produces within us a sense of awe and continuous inquiry. Once we know this, we can translate it into a conversation and mutual discussion that appeals to the phenomenological world of our students. I will try to illustrate this with a "stone."

If I were to be with a group of elementary students and simply pick up a stone, I could begin to ask: "How old do you think this is?" "Where do you think it came from?" "How might it travel to get here?" "Who or what may have used it?" "For what purpose?" "What might happen to it after we leave?" "Is it lifeless?" "How was it made?" "Why does it have color?" "What does it remind you of?" "How could we use it?" "Should we leave it?" And more.

Or I might just say, "What a dumb looking rock," and throw it away.

Curiosity and wonder come from our imagination and emotions. They are produced by us for us. They can be learned and expanded or blunted and retarded. Nothing is mysterious until we touch it with our minds and feelings. All students have this capacity, but it is a capacity that is only realized under the proper conditions and facilitation.

Another approach is to find out from students what currently appeals to their curiosity and explorative nature. Then use this information to create topics and learning activities for their choice. Some helpful discussion questions might be:

What do you like to fantasize about?

What's even scary to just think about?

What seems mysterious to you?

If you could choose anyone to have a conversation with, who would it be? What would it be about?

What kind of books, movies, or television programs make you think?

Write the five questions you would most like to have answered.

What would you like to do more often, more intensely, etc.?

What would you like to know more about?

What about the future seems unpredictable?

What about the past seems strange?

Imagine a beautiful moment. What is it? What happens?

What's the best thing that could happen to you?

What makes you worry?

If you could have a single power, what would it be?

The list is endless. Using it can make teaching exciting and help students toward motivated involvement as well as self-actualization.

Strategy 2: *Encourage divergent thinking and creativity in the learning process.* Creativity is a way of thinking and acting or making something that is original for the individual and valued by that person or others.[11] *Divergent thinking* is a process of exploring and considering many possible solutions or answers to a problem or question; *convergent thinking* results in only a single solution or answer. If a student is asked to give a specific date for a war, she/he will have to think convergently, but if the student is asked to discuss possible results of the war, she/he will think divergently. Divergent thinking stimulates creativity and meets the need for self-actualization because students have the opportunity to consider possibilities, explore their unique perceptions, evaluate their thinking, and expand their awareness.

Students enjoy playing with ideas, exploring their interests, and inventing things, both concrete and abstract. We can facilitate their "need to actualize" by:

1. Providing free periods when materials and books are available to students to follow their own pursuits.

2. Accepting notions of intuition, guessing, and estimation in learning as valid means to approach problem solving.

3. Accepting fantasy as a way to explore the known and unknown.

4. Allowing students to go at their own pace and "flow" in learning activities they are excited about and interested in. (We feel this when "we can't put a book down" or "hate to leave" a concert, a dance, a party, etc. It's the feeling of being able to go on and on and on—one of the sheerest pleasures of learning.)

5. Letting students figure out their own way of doing things when they prefer to.

6. Asking questions that begin with *just suppose* (Just suppose there was no money. What would we do?) or *imagine that* (Imagine that you could advise the president. What would you suggest?) or *what would happen if* (What would happen if time didn't exist?) or *in how many different ways* (In how many different ways could you show people that you cared for them?).

7. Sometimes making work playful and learning artistic and thinking emotional and not always falsely separating one from the other. (I don't have an easy "how to" guide for this suggestion, but I do know how I do it for myself. I take the most tedious thing I have to teach and concentrate on making it fun. Sometimes this is

very difficult and demands much planning, but I usually can do it. And when I do, I know I'm home free, because the rest is possible.)

Strategy 3: *Provide the opportunity for self-discovery through freedom of choice in the learning situation with emphasis on problem solving, experimentation, and self-evaluation.* Some part of any curriculum can be offered to students "to learn about themselves by learning about something else." They are to choose the topic or project to insure self-commitment. After this criterion has been met, there is opportunity for exploration, invention, and/or experimentation in the process so that they can test their insight, hunches, and feelings. The project can be open ended so that they can feel their own power of completion or the right to say Yes or No to their own learning. Finally, they are to establish their own criteria for evaluation and acceptance, giving them a sense of their own standards and satisfaction. In this enterprise we take the role of *consultant*. We can give them knowledgeable information and suggestions but no "hassle." A log or diary may be kept to record their feelings and sense of progress. This project can culminate in a discussion with the student to determine what she/he has learned and to explore the meaning that this process had for her/his appreciation of her/his potential.

In any self-actualization—related activity, student impulses are desired and welcomed rather than rejected and feared. With self-direction, student self-understanding is fostered by active problem solving in which the best preparation for the future is living in worthwhile involvement in the present. Students are not asked to be what other people want them to be but to be what they have chosen to be.

Chapter 4	**Stimulation:**
	Continuing What
	Is Worthwhile

The man is sitting alone at a campfire. As the flame dwindles, the scene moves to the bushes and trees behind him. A twig snaps and leaves rustle. A large dark figure appears and immediately disappears. In the background an eerie throbbing sound begins to grow louder and louder. As the scene shifts back to the campfire a strong wind emerges taking the last glimmer of light from the fire with it. All is shadows with only the sound of erratic human breathing and whistling air funneling from a darkened core. And then . . .

Stimulating? Attention-getting? Scary? Why? It could be the beginning of a myriad of television programs and motion pictures that our culture currently "enjoys" as entertaining. My goal in writing this paragraph was to gain attention and excite—to involve the reader with a piece of stimulating writing. Television and movie directors do it consistently with "teasers"—fast-paced flashes of adventure, mystery, and love to engage their viewers and "hook" them at the beginning of their programs and films.

How is this done? Usually with a glimpse or series of scenes that builds up action, adventure, or interest but remains unfinished or incomplete. There is often some form of stirring music in the background to accentuate what is seen. These "teasers" are planned to get our attention, momentarily increase our involvement, and make us stick around to see what's going to happen to bring closure to this exciting beginning. Even local news programs begin with this format—only this time it's that happy-go-lucky trio of buddies: the newscaster, the sportscaster, and the weathercaster who gleefully look at one another as they introduce the highlights of their broadcast with folksy humor and then assault us with the tragedies and thunderstorms of our daily lives.

But is this what education should become? And does stimulation simply mean excitement? Yes and no. Yes, sometimes learning can be exciting, and we have much to gain from understanding the methods of television and movie programming. However, to be consistently exciting is not a goal that I advocate for teachers. We are not in the entertainment business. And to be constantly exciting means to be continuously "on"—to be playing a part, carrying on a role, or orchestrating a series of images and limiting the real connection with our students as persons with feelings, vulnerability, and human needs. In fact, constant excitement may be detrimental to student motivation. It may keep students in a passive, recipient state as television often does, leaving the student lethargic and dependent on someone to make life exciting. It may blur thinking and prevent scholarly questioning and reflective thought. It may even prevent student interest from developing because its pace carries the participant *through* the activity before the student can develop any involvement *within* it.

Stimulation can and should be many things. It can be exciting. It can also be interesting and frustrating. While it may stir, spur, and invigorate, it may also tingle, trouble, and irritate. To put it colloquially, "it's a mixed bag." Essentially, and by definition, it is an optimal change in a person's perception or experience with her/his environment. In my opinion it is a human physiological need and basic to any continual involvement in learning. *Stimulation has to occur to sustain student learning behavior.* Students will begin many learning activities because they feel they need them, or because they have a positive attitude toward them, but they will not continue to attend and be involved unless they find the learning stimulating. If the learning is not stimulating, they will be *distracted* by something more stimulating—a friend, a mischievous act, a daydream, etc. In many ways, school is nothing more than a setting where different forms of stimulation compete for student attention. When the stimulating is done by the teacher and is approved by the principal and the community, we call it "learning." When the stimulating is done by other students and is not approved by the principal and the community, we label it "a discipline problem."

Stimulation is hard to put a finger on. Like morality, it tends to be relative. Just as what is right and good for one person may not be so for another person, what is exciting and interesting for one student may not be so for another student. What is stimulating to a person is a function of the person's developmental stage, cultural background, experiential history, previous experience with the stimulus, and expectancy for the situation. With 30 students, there are 30 possibilities. No wonder teachers age just thinking of the word!

It is ironic that the need for stimulation, which is so basic and profound for people, is also rare in our individual abilities to stimulate.

Who can command the attention of everyone? Who can for 30 hours per week sustain the interest of 25 people? This is the average class. It is not easy. The ability to consistently stimulate is so uncommon in our society that I think it is reflected in our basic economics. The highest salaried people in this culture are our entertainers. If what we are willing to pay is a barometer of what we need, they who can stimulate the largest numbers receive our dollars as well as our devotion.

What then are the possibilities for teachers to be more stimulating? Good news. There are quite a few. However, there are very few general rules that give consistent specific guidance. One that will permeate all the subfactors and strategies that follow is *to match the learning process* (whether it be materials, activities, assignments, questions, discussions, etc.) *with the cognitive, emotional, and physical–motor levels of the student*. This principle is based on the work of Piaget, Hunt, and other significant learning theorists. Stated in more simplified terms: Students are usually interested in anything that is a bit more novel and/or difficult than what they already know. If they experience something that is too new or is too difficult or unfamiliar, they may be confused, frustrated, or frightened. If they experience something that is not new or is too simple or merely repetitive, they may be repulsed, bored, or restless. Graphically this may be illustrated in Figure 8.

For example, if an average fifth grader says that her/his favorite subject is animals and we give this student a college text on zoology, she/he may be enthusiastic during initial attempts to read, but will soon bog down and probably compensate by looking at the

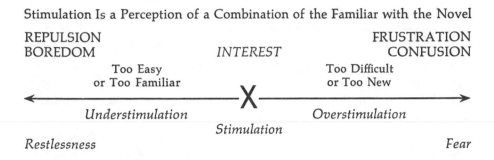

Figure 8

Stimulation Is a Perception of a Combination of the Familiar with the Novel

REPULSION   FRUSTRATION
BOREDOM   *INTEREST*   CONFUSION
        Too Easy   Too Difficult
     or Too Familiar   or Too New

←————————————————— X —————————————————→

      Understimulation   *Overstimulation*
                     Stimulation
Restlessness   *Fear*

pictures before frustration and/or confusion sets in. If we give the student a book on animals written at the first-grade level with sentences such as, "See the dog," and, "Isn't the cat cute?" making up the text, she/he will easily become bored or perhaps be offended by its simplistic nature. A book on animals written at the fourth-, fifth-, or sixth-grade level should maintain the student's interest.

In a similar vein, if a person who is accustomed to putting 150-piece puzzles together is asked to put a 1000-piece puzzle together, this person may feel overwhelmed and confused. If this same person were given a 10-piece puzzle, she/he might easily feel bored or repulsed by its elementary structure. However, this person should be interested in working on a 200-piece puzzle.

If I give you another one of these examples, you will probably become bored so I will stop.

Another rule of thumb is that there is usually an inverted U-shaped relationship between stimulation and performance. I have modified a model created by Korman[1] to illustrate this concept in Figure 9.

What this means is that students think and work best on assignments, projects, and learning activities when they are moderately stimulated. If there is too little stimulation in the learning activity, they will be easily distracted so as to increase their stimulation level. I maintain that discipline problems arise more from the need for stimulation than from any evil or immoral source. If students are too highly stimulated, they will dissipate energy and attention to lower their stimulation level so that they can concentrate on the task at

Figure 9

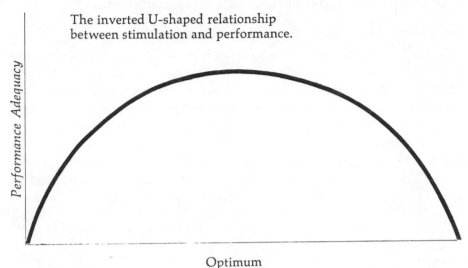

The inverted U-shaped relationship
between stimulation and performance.

Performance Adequacy

Low Stimulation Level	Optimum (Moderate) Stimulation Level	High Stimulation Level
Some behavior will be devoted to increasing stimulation level as well as to task demands.	Optimum attention paid to task demands.	Some behavior will be devoted to decreasing stimulation level as well as to task demands.

hand. It is no surprise that college students take tranquilizers before final exams and that high school students can "choke" in competitive academic as well as athletic contests. Giggling, talking loudly, biting pencils, shaking legs, dropping books, and taking deep breaths are common methods that students use to decrease the extra tension from overstimulation during tests, report givings, oral exams, and argumentative discussions.

Probably a vital and relaxed atmosphere is best for optimal performance on learning tasks. However, we are not always seeking "optimal performance" in education. Sometimes we just want to have fun, release energy, relate to one another, and share emotions. High stimulation may be an excellent facilitator, but dullness and boredom are seldom partners to anything of value.

The ways in which we introduce and connect our learning activities are pinpoints of potential stimulation for students. Let's take a closer look at this never-ending teacher function.

Introduction and Connection of Learning Activities

One way to view daily education is to see it as a unit with many subunits or as a game with many subgames or "plays." Just as a baseball game has innings that are divided into outs and even strikes and just as a football game has quarters that are divided into downs and plays, so a classroom learning unit has topics divided into subtopics, presentations, discussions, questions, and answers. Each of these particular learning activities is enhanced when properly introduced and connected to previous and future learning activities. A teacher may easily introduce and connect 15 subtopics or learning units in an hour! A question-and-answer session could fluently touch upon 25 units of study in a 40-minute session. Therefore, it is of maximum importance to student motivation to effectively introduce or connect each new topic or activity.

Strategy 1: *Use focusing methods or materials to draw the student's attention to the new learning activity or topic.* This means that each time we reach another subunit of learning or change in topic, we do something to renew and invigorate student attention to it. This can be as simple as asking a relevant question or as complex as taking a special field trip. Some stimulating methods are:

1. *Employ basic attraction techniques.*

   a. Using visual and audio aids—pictures, posters, slides, tapes, films, etc.

   b. Changing voice tone or amplification—speaking softer or louder, more joyfully or sadder, etc.

   c. Hesitating or pausing—a brief silence can be amazingly attention getting.

   d. Changing body position or language—standing up, sitting down, moving to the center of the room, raising hands, frowning, smiling, etc.

   e. Asking relevant questions—"How many have ever . . .?" "What do you think is . . .?" "When was the last time . . .?" And so on.

f. Calling on students—to help, to move, to observe, to question, to relate, etc.

g. Creating suspense—"I'll bet you can't imagine what's coming next." "This is really tricky." "This even scares me." "I don't know how this is going to turn out." "Sometimes I think it's magic when . . . ." And so on.

2. *Create an expectancy or organizing context for the ideas, experiences, or information that follows.*

a. Using advance organizers—anything that organizes or integrates the subject or material that a student will study (e.g., handing out a set of definitions, passing out an outline of the topic to be studied, presenting a graphic chart of interrelated concepts, etc.).

b. Telling what the new topic relates to—it may continue a previous lesson, it may be the last item studied, it may introduce a new unit, it may be helpful for a future activity, etc.

c. Supporting the practical relevancy of the new topic—show how it helps the student to understand her/his identity, meet a basic need, gain a vocational skill, etc.

3. *Relate the new topic or learning activity to current student interests*—movies, television programs, sports figures and events, common folk heroes, newspaper articles, local cultural events, etc. For example,

"This is the 17th-century version of *Jaws*."

"Let's practice our math skills and compute the batting averages of our team."

"See how this might compare with Watergate."

Strategy 2: *For recitation and discussion, use Kounin's[3] positive group alerting cues.* Positive group alerting cues are what a teacher uses to keep nonreciters on their toes while another student is talking or before the selection of a new discussant. Some of these are:

1. *Creating "suspense" before calling on a student to respond*—pause and look around to "bring students in" before selecting one; say, "I wonder who can. . ." before calling on a person to answer a question.

2. *Keeping students uncertain with regard to whom will be called on next*—pick them randomly so that no one knows whether she/he will be called next or not.

3. *Asking for a show of hands in response to a question before selecting a respondent.*

4. *Alerting nonperformers during a discussion that they may be asked to explain or evaluate someone else's response during a discussion.*

5. *Avoiding prepicking a respondent before the question is asked.* In other words, ask the question, wait 3–5 seconds while everyone considers the answer, and then pick or allow a student to respond.

Variety

"Variety is the spice of life!" The assumption behind this statement is that variety is good. We should have more variety in teaching to stimulate students. This is why words like "innovate," "diversity," and "change" have such strong appeal in educational jargon. Maybe not. My review of the literature and research does not support variety "for the sake of variety."

To simply mix or change subject matter, teaching style, student configuration, or learning materials does not necessarily improve stimulation or student motivation. I cannot even say that constant lecturing is a poor teaching technique. (My two finest teachers tended to lecture most of the time!) In general, variety in learning seems like a good idea, but how it is done remains the important question—and the illusive mystery.

Pace, tempo, and blend seem to be critical factors in creating the type of variety that is conducive to student motivation. Simply mixing different seasonings does not create an excellent meal, but tastefully blending various seasonings does. Combining notes is not music; in fact, it may be only noise until those notes are placed in proper tempo, rhythm, and coordination. So it is with variety in teaching. We know we must vary what we present and the style in which we present it, as well as the style in which students receive it, but no formula for how to vary anything in learning is guaranteed to stimulate. In fact, when a student is making progress in any mode of learning, she/he may resist and resent any change we attempt to facilitate—and rightfully so. Therefore, my first suggestion:

Strategy 1: *Whenever possible, let the learner control the pace, choices, and changes in her/his learning activity.* Boredom is aversive. Students will not let themselves remain bored and disinterested. They know when they need a change better than we do. Yet, I know that we must continue to evaluate for their learning progress, involvement—activity level, and general exposure to new learning. However, it is within these parameters that we can structure learning environments that allow for *more* choice and self-direction. Individualized education, the open classroom model, and Montessori methods are some major educational approaches that support this view.

In my opinion, we make a mistake to make students totally dependent on us for their motivational state. By providing learning centers, self-guiding materials, learning options, and different learning modalities—i.e., reading materials vs. audiotapes vs. films vs. project activity—we can accomplish the same immediate goal and work toward the larger goal of letting students *learn how to learn.*

Strategy 2: *Use movement, voice, body language, pauses, and props to vitalize and accentuate classroom presentations.* The best way to begin is to make an audiovisual tape of yourself teaching a lesson. Choose an ordinary presentation for half of the tape and one with your "best stuff" for the second half. Then compare the difference between the two halves using the following criteria:

1. *Body movement:*
    a. How often do you move?
    b. In what direction?
    c. Are you among your students?
    d. Are you predictable in your movements?

You are a stimulus and a stimulus that does **not** move or "connect" with students draws very little attention.

2. *Voice:*
    a. What is the tone of your voice?
    b. How often does it change?
    c. When does it change?
    d. How is your voice used for emphasis, emotion, and support of your subject?

e. What would it be like to listen to you and not see you?

Very few of us are Demosthenes or Walter Cronkite. We are the best we have to offer. The question is, Are you using your voice to its best advantage? The voice continuously "colors" our message. Avoid being grey.

3. *Body language:*
    a. Do you use gestures?
    b. If so, what kind? When?
    c. How animated is your face?
    d. What would it be like to see you and not hear you? (Turn off the sound.)
    e. What is the relationship of your body language to student questions, responses, and behavior?

Body language is often the (not so) hidden message behind any presentation. It is what students use as a base for their intuitive sense about the subject presented. It reveals enthusiasm and positive regard as well as boredom and rejection.

4. *Pauses:*
    a. When do you pause?
    b. What happens?
    c. How long do you remain silent?
    d. For what purpose do you use silence?

According to Shostak,[4] many teachers lack the ability to use pauses effectively. We seem to fear what might happen if the sound of our voices stops for even a moment. This fear leads us to use "teacher talk" not as a means of effective communication but as a defense mechanism to maintain classroom control. He lists numerous ways that pauses or silence can enhance our teaching. Some of them are:

—To break informational segments into smaller pieces for better understanding.

—To capture attention by contrasting sound with silence.

—To signal students to prepare for the next teacher action.

—To emphasize an important point.

—To provide time for thinking about a question or formulating an answer.

—To create suspense or expectation.

—To provide a model for listening behavior.

5. *Props:*

   a. What do you use to visually or concretely involve your students? When? How?

   b. How can students "see" and "feel" what you are talking about?

   c. What are the relative sizes, colors, vividness, and novelty values of your props?

   d. Do you present material through as many sensory modalities as you can?

   e. How smoothly are props introduced and withdrawn?

We know that, in general, using more than one sense in learning facilitates motivation and the learning process. Visual and auditory stimulation is superior to either one alone, and visual–auditory–motor stimulation is superior to visual–auditory. This may be a summation effect or simply give more clarity by involving more senses. That is why textbooks have pictures and films have sound. To stand up and "do it on our own" may only increase the probabilities in favor of the liabilities in our presentation.

I know that to ask you to view and critique yourself in terms of classroom teaching can be very threatening. I resisted it myself. However, I know of no stronger or more powerful means of self-improvement for facilitating the motivation of students. If you accept any suggestions from this book, I ask you to accept this one first.[5] Make it a mutual effort and invite a couple of professional colleagues to join you in this endeavor. It only takes three to have a seminar. Be critical, but keep it light.

Strategy 3: *Shift interaction between yourself and the students and between the students themselves during classroom presentations.* No matter how good we are, students do get tired of listening to us. As we lecture or demonstrate to the class, it is advisable to create a dialogue with our students at points that seem appropriate to the lesson at hand. We may ask their opinions, or ask for feedback, or engage their help, or simply acknowledge their feelings and consideration for the matter being discussed. Unless it's a sermon, any really good lecture is always a dialogue, either covert or overt.

During presentations, we can also redirect the questions and comments of one student to other students. "What do you think about Zena's remark, Andy?" "Phil, how would you approach what Stella just said?" By fluently channeling discussion from ourselves to students, and back, or to other students, as the lesson or mood dictates, we can help to create a rhythm that maintains high student attention and motivation.

Strategy 4: *Change the style as well as the content of the learning activities.* So often as a student, I have had teachers who religiously changed the subject matter but never varied the style. As a fifth grader I would come to class and immediately sit down and begin writing the chalkboard assignment. In 15 minutes, I would be asked to take out my spelling workbook and respond to its contents in writing. After 40 minutes, I would be asked to take out my math book and begin to copy problems. At this time, I would start to feel a violent urge to use the bathroom which probably had nothing to do with my food or liquid intake that morning. College was only worse. Fifty minutes of listening to a biology lecture, followed by fifty minutes of listening to a psychology lecture, followed by fifty minutes of listening to a history lecture, followed by an urge to scream and run. We had $70 million of the finest buildings in the city designed by some of the greatest architects in the nation, and it all could have been replaced by a microphone and folding chairs.

So . . . please change style as well as content in classroom activities. This can mean varying the thinking process from convergent to divergent thinking; varying the presentation process from lecturing to discussion; varying the group configuration from entire class activities to small group work; varying the student behavior from writing to large muscle movement games; and varying the location from anywhere inside the class to anywhere outside it.

Strategy 5: *Use closure techniques to help the student organize her/his attention to the end of a unit or subunit.* There is no doubt that student attention is enhanced by structure in the learning process.

As we have mentioned, there are many subunits of learning in daily teaching. If we help students to be alert to the ending of these various subunits, we aid their attention and avoid confusion. Some techniques that may be helpful in this manner are:

1. *Reviewing the basic concepts or principles contained in the subunit of learning*—"Now that we have discussed why World War II ended, let's review the major reasons we touched upon."

2. *Allowing for clarification at the end of a lesson or exercise*—"We seem to have completed this section on air pollution. Are there any further questions that need to be addressed?"

3. *Allowing for feedback*—"Now that we've practiced this form of communication, how do you feel about what you've done?"

4. *Consolidating relationships*—"We've really had fun working on comedy, but how does what we have just learned relate to what we did when we were studying tragedy?"

5. *Encouraging transfer*—"Now that we've studied what the moon is, how do you think this has prepared us for our next unit on the sun?"

6. *Taking advantage of spontaneous closure that arises from the unsuspected dynamics of classroom behavior and unique situations*—The class has just spontaneously applauded a student's response. "I can't think of a better way to end this discussion. Let's take a break."

Interest and Involvement

To me, involvement is any time a student is actively participating psychologically or physically in the learning process. By actively, I mean that the student is *aware* of her/his relationship to the learning process. The student's attention, interest, and physical reactions are focused and readily a part of the learning activity. In a very literal sense, the learning process cannot continue without student reactions or responses. This can range from simple discussion to educational games to intricate role playing. By functional definition, involvement means that the student is motivated because she/he is aware and actively participating in the learning, whereas in passive learning situations, the instruction may occur as in lecturing, but student motivation and involvement may be absent.

Interest is the student's mental and emotional willingness to get involved in the learning process. It depends on the student's experience with the learning activity and the pleasantness of that experience. Essentially, positive exposure to any topic in which the student can experience some degree of success and make progress in the learning experience will build interest. We can recognize current student interests by being alert to their culture, friends, social and play activities, and previous learning experiences. These we can use to build upon and to introduce new learning activities. But we also must create new interests by providing opportunities for learning in which students can be initially successful and stimulated.

Strategy 1: *Guarantee success and pleasure at the beginning of any new learning experience.* Make it quick, light, vivid, active, and fun. The motto for this approach is the student feeling, "I can't resist." In order to prepare, ask yourself these three questions:

1. What is at least one important idea or significant insight that that students can learn from the first lesson?
2. How can I make it fun or exciting?
3. How can I stop so they will want more?

For example, a friend of mine was beginning a unit on mammals for third graders. For his first lesson he brought a puppy to class. He began by simply bringing the group into a closed circle on the floor with the puppy roaming at will in the middle. His first question was, "How is this puppy different from a lizard?" The class took it from there. After 50 minutes, he had great difficulty bringing the session to a close due to student interest and excitement. The mammal unit was on its way.

Strategy 2: *Find out what student interests are and relate learning to them.* At the beginning of any course or class find out what your students' interests are. This can be done by having students respond verbally or in writing to a series of questions aimed at securing this information. Some possible items are:

1. What's your favorite movie or television program?
2. What kind of books do you read for pleasure?
3. If you could have three people over for dinner, who would they be?

4. What do you like to do with your free time?

5. What are some hobbies you enjoy or think you would enjoy?

Save or record these answers for each student, and use them to organize projects, create questions, select topics, design lessons, devise examples, etc.

Strategy 3: *Use humor, examples, analogies, stories, and questions to facilitate the active participation of each student in your lectures and demonstrations.* Whenever we lecture or demonstrate, we have a naturally passive audience. What brings them to life and can get them mentally and emotionally involved in our presentation is their identification with us or our topic.

Humor is a sharing of emotion. It provides a common emotional release that is stimulating and attention getting. I cannot tell anyone how to be funny. But I have a hunch that many of us do not use humor because of fear—fear of seeming stupid, fear of losing control, fear of missing the punch line, fear that no one will laugh. Very logical but very inhibiting—and dull. Take a chance. See what happens.

Examples are the bread and butter of any good presentation. They should be clear, identifiable to the listener, vivid in detail and description, and to the point. They allow for clarification and identification with the topic by the listener. They ease the burden of concentration for the audience and provide time for reflection and application. Use them liberally, especially with abstract subjects such as science and philosophy.

Analogies are examples that enhance clarification by showing new ideas and principles in already understandable form and context. If we say that being a teacher in charge of a high school lunchroom is a difficult task, we are logically clear. But if we say that being the responsible teacher in a high school lunchroom is like being the only police officer at a stadium rock concert, we have added zest to the meaning.

Stories, especially when personal to the teacher or class, allow for identification with the topic as well as for elaboration and vivid imaginative appeal. Like a good picture they are worth a thousand words and add color and emphasis to the meaning of what is being done.

Questions can be asked to heighten involvement even when time or group size does not allow them to be specifically answered. For example, questions may ask the student to reflect upon or mentally participate in the topic at hand: "How many of you have tried this?" "How do you think you would answer this question?" "Think of an experience that is similar to the one I have just described." "What would you do if you were in this predicament?"

The main idea in all situations where the student is likely to be a passive recipient of learning is not to allow that passivity to dominate. Each of the above suggestions can limit indifferent learning and heighten student involvement.

Strategy 4: *Whenever possible, make student reaction and involvement an essential part of the learning process.* In this approach, the goal is to allow the student to figuratively or literally "step into and become a part" of the learning activity. When the student is an inclusive element in the learning process, it is much more difficult for her/his attention to wander or for stimulus distraction to occur. We also know that the active reaction of students is the fundamental basis for learning. Principles or ideas can be presented, but it is the students' outlining, questioning, problem solving, discussing, and applying that cement the understanding and learning for them. Here are some ways to facilitate involvement.

1. *Create as many learning situations as possible where students are active participants through processes[6] such as games[7], role playing, exercises, discussion, team projects, and simulation.*

2. *Encourage overt bodily activity by providing the opportunity for manipulation of materials or the construction of models, displays, art works, etc.; request detailed observation and recording of experiments, student behavior, field studies, etc.*

3. *Use active investigation methods such as experiments, puzzles, problems, etc.*

4. *Allow students to evaluate their learning as this is a natural interest which is facilitated by the need for self-esteem.*

Questions

Every time we pose a question to students, we are providing a stimulus. How stimulating that stimulus is depends upon the kind of question we ask. John Dewey wrote that thinking itself is questioning. In my opinion, a good question not only provokes thought but also helps to elicit feelings as well—e.g., "What is amazing about this story?" Any time we ask a question, we have the opportunity to spontaneously stimulate our students. It is the quality and timing of the question that can determine its stimulus value.

Unfortunately, educational research indicates that although most teachers ask many questions, these questions are usually the kind that depend on rote memory to be correctly answered. When we also consider that some research studies show that elementary school teachers may ask as many as 348 questions per day, with only an average of one second given to students to respond, it seems that teacher questioning may often prompt very little student thinking or emotion.[8]

Bloom's taxonomy[9] is a good system for classifying questions and organizing strategies to enhance the stimulation value of teacher inquiry methods. This taxonomy has six levels by which teachers can present to students questions that require a variety of stimulating thought processes.

1. *Knowledge questions*—These usually depend on rote memory and require students to recall or recognize information: "Who invented the automobile?"

2. *Comprehension questions*—These require students to interpret, compare, or explain what they have learned: "Could you explain in your own words the meaning of this definition?"

3. *Application questions*—These require students to use what they have learned to solve problems: "According to our definition of creativity, which of the following behaviors would be considered creative?"

4. *Analysis questions*—These require students to identify causes and motives as well as to infer, deduce, and generalize: "Why do people respond differently to similar frustrations?"

5. *Synthesis questions*—These require students to think divergently (creatively) in solving problems, producing ideas, and developing any kind of intellectual response: "What would an ideal modern city be like to you?"

6. *Evaluation questions*—These require students to judge or appraise anything they are perceiving: "Which president since 1936 has been most effective?"

Strategy 1: *Limit the use of knowledge questions and selectively increase the use of comprehension, application, analysis, synthesis, and evaluation questions.*[10]

This can be seen as an avoidance and approach process for teacher inquiry methods. The words listed in Figure 10 are *key initiators* for questioning processes that can enhance or limit the stimulation value of whatever we ask our students.

Figure 10[11]

KEY INITIATORS FOR QUESTIONING PROCESSES

AVOID   *APPROACH*

(Knowledge-Oriented)   *(Comprehension-Oriented)*
Define   Describe
Identify   Compare
Recall   Illustrate
Recognize   Interpret
Who?   Rephrase
What?   Reorder
Where?   Contrast
When?   Differentiate
                                          Explain

                                          (Application-Oriented)
                                          Apply
                                          Solve
                                              (only one answer
                                              is correct)
                                          Classify
                                          Choose
                                          Select

APPROACH

(Application-Oriented)
Use
Employ

(Analysis-Oriented)
Analyze
Give motive, cause, or reason
Conclude
Infer
Distinguish
Deduce
Detect
Why?

(Synthesis-Oriented)
Solve
    (more than one
    answer correct)
Predict
Draw
Construct
Produce
Originate
Propose
Plan
Design
Synthesize
Combine
Develop
Create

(Evaluation-Oriented)
Judge

APPROACH

(Evaluation-Oriented)
Argue
Decide
Appraise
Evaluate
What's your opinion?
Agree or disagree?
Better or worse?
Right or wrong?

An interesting approach to self-improvement might be to have an observer categorize your questions for a day to: (1) see how many you ask; (2) identify the key initiation word(s) and categorize their orientation; and (3) rate your questions as to how well they stimulate thinking and discussion. You can then study the observer's data and make decisions regarding how you might want to affirm or alter your questioning skills. Synthesis questions have the most potential for creative stimulation, but are often the least used.

Strategy 2: *Employ M. Sadker and D. Sadker's[12] suggestions for improving the quality of questioning skills that enhance student responsiveness.*

1. *Increase the "wait time" between your question and the reception of a student response.* At least 3 to 5 seconds seems appropriate, and maybe even longer for those questions at the analysis, synthesis, and evaluation levels. This allows students to think and can result in more imaginative answers, participation by more students, and greater confidence on the part of students in what they do say.

2. *Avoid teacher echo*—repeating portions of student responses to a question. This tends to arbitrarily conclude what the student has said and dulls further reflection.

3. *Avoid pressuring students to "think" about what you have asked.* Students usually resent this form of indirect intimidation which implies that they don't readily understand in the first place. The question you ask should provide its own provocative stimulation.

4. *Avoid frequent evaluative comments*—"That's good," "Okay," "Excellent," etc. Even though these may be positive, they make you the judge and jury, deciding what's right or wrong. Acknowledgment, appreciation, and transition responses such as, "Now, I see how you understand it," or, "Thanks for that comment," or, "Well, that must mean . . . [followed by a new question]," tend to have greater chances of continuing discussion and thinking.

5. *Avoid "Yes . . . but" reactions to student answers.* Essentially this is a rejection of the student's idea. The "but" cancels out what precedes it and affirms what follows it—e.g., "Yes, I think that might work, but here is a better way."

6. *Use nonverbal language to increase student responses.* Smiling, nodding, moving toward or away, leaning forward, and eye contact are all ways to involve students and acknowledge their answers. A caution—too much eye contact can "rivet" students to us and inhibit student-to-student discussion. Sometimes a short comment such as, "Why don't you tell Eric what you think?" can facilitate student-to-student communication.

7. *Probe student answers to stimulate more thinking and/or discussion.* Probing questions or comments require students to provide more support, to be clearer or more accurate, and to offer greater specificity or originality—e.g., "How did you arrive at that conclusion?" "What are some other possibilities?" "I don't quite understand." "Explain a bit more."

Disequilibrium

Most learning is usually purposive. Students have a goal in mind when they are learning. They want to "understand" something. They want to practice and improve a skill. They want to "solve" a problem. They want to gain a new insight. Whenever they are confronted with something new or different from what they already know, they feel a tension or need to fit it into what they do know. This "tension" can be called a state of disequilibrium. When they "fit in" or assimilate and accommodate the new learning, the tension is reduced, and equilibrium or a sense of balance is felt by the learner.

This state of tension is a motivating force. So when a student knows that $5 \times 6 = 30$ and is asked for the first time what 5×7 equals, she/he is motivated to fit this new multiplication fact into her or his repertoire of knowledge and find the answer. In a similar vein, if a student knows what makes a person fall asleep, she/he will probably be interested in knowing what makes a person wake up as well.

What this means for us is that whenever we can produce or facilitate a state of disequilibrium in our students, we have a motivated group of learners to contend with. According to Bigge,[13] student involvement is at its best when student perplexity is just short of frustration. Therefore, whenever we confront students with information or processes that are different, novel, contrasting, or discrepant from what they already know or have experienced, their motivational pumps are primed for action.

Strategy 1: *Introduce contrasting or disturbing data and information.* This leaves students with a positive sense of dissatisfaction for what they know. Their basic response is, "How come?" This was first brought to my attention by an excellent fifth-grade science teacher I experienced as a student. Every time we started a class with her, she would present an intriguing question: "If rain falls out of clouds, how come clouds do not fall as well?" or, "The moon is round like a ball. A ball rolls. Does the moon roll across the sky?" With these kinds of questions, she had us involved immediately. The same is true for controversial speakers. We may not like what they say, but we do listen to what is said. Every teacher can do this for any subject. The only limit is our imagination.

Strategy 2: *Permit a humane degree of student mistakes and frustrations.* Isn't this what problem solving and experimentation are all about? The challenge is in the possibility of achievement, not in the certainty of success. I am always taken with the story of Edison and his Menlo Park colleagues in their one hundred plus attempts at inventing the first light bulb. Can you imagine the ninety-ninth time when they gathered in that little room, threw the switch, and watched that little bulb pop? Nonetheless, they persevered and finally succeeded.

So let students run into some dead ends and experience some difficulty with their projects and experiments. A word of caution—I do believe this kind of motivation is dependent on a significant amount of previous successful experience with the subject matter, as well as on a positive self-concept. Students who have not been successful in previous endeavors or who have low self-concepts will not readily be challenged by mistakes and frustration.

Strategy 3: *Play the devil's advocate.* Do it with selectivity and decency. I never liked those teachers who did it in a patronizing and vindictive manner.

Strategy 4: *Facilitate the search and recognition of incomplete Gestalts.* This is commonly known as the "Zeigarnik effect." In 1927 Zeigarnik demonstrated that learners tend to recall unfinished tasks and to forget completed ones. A Gestalt psychologist, she theorized that a "tension system" builds up in the person until the task is finished. Incomplete tasks leave us with a desire to get back and finalize our work. This is why serial movies and unfinished novels may have such a strong attraction for us to "find out how they end."

I believe a similar motivational system operates behind the old entertainers' adage of "Always leave them wanting more." Their encores never seem to be enough, and we walk away gasping for another chance to "see" them. What this means for us in our work with students is that when a particular lesson seems to be going very well and does have a natural beginning and end, we may be wise to interrupt the completion so as to prevent closure, and thereby facilitate student motivation for the next opportunity. I like to do this with exciting involvement activities such as games, role playing, and discussions.

However, the opposite effect can occur with undesirable learning activities that seem to have "no end in sight." Students tune out or distract themselves because the "suffering" seems to have no limit, and they want to avoid a continual aversive experience. (Just remember what you did at the last luncheon, meeting, or graduation when you had to sit and listen to a boring speaker who seemed to go on and on and . . . .) In those situations where we know that our subject matter is difficult or trying or repetitive, I think we are wise to admit this to our students and to place a time limit on the experience. "I know this stuff seems repetitive, but I feel it's important to what we are doing, and we'll be done with it in 30 minutes." My experience is that students appreciate the honesty and will "hang in there" with me. Coaches do this with difficult drills, and Madison Avenue has learned the value of a good 20-second commercial. We would be wise to take heed.

Strategy 5: *Be unpredictable to the degree that students enjoy your spontaneity with a sense of security.* The surest death of a stimulating teacher is when her or his students can smugly predict her or his classroom behavior. When our students know exactly what we're going to do and when we're going to do it, we have lost their sense of interest and anticipation. This transfers learning from a secure routine to a boring rut. Students want something new in what we do and say. To be totally predictable means not only that we have stopped being spontaneous but also that we have stopped learning and are trapped by the ease or safety of our own habits.

Anytime I hear a teacher say, "I'm bored with my job," I know that among other things that person has stopped being innovative or spontaneous. What such a statement means for that teacher's students is that they are probably bored as well. Any relationship, whether between a teacher and a student, between a husband and a wife, or between a friend and a friend, must have some unpredictability to be vital. Growth as a teacher or an individual means change and temporary loss of predictability.

Some ways to maintain a positive sense of unpredictability for our students are:

1. *While teaching, stay aware of the moment and situation, trusting your perception and feelings to do what seems appropriate.* Spontaneity is determined more by intuition than by reflection, and definitely by giving ourselves permission to make mistakes.

2. *Stay in touch with the subculture of your students.* Their needs are usually basic, but their social activities and influences are constantly evolving. Our awareness of who they are and what they enjoy can give our approach to teaching a constant source of new examples, interests, and viewpoints.

3. *Be professionally up to date in your discipline.* Every subject area and teaching level have a professional organization. Local and national conventions, as well as journals, provide information on innovative approaches, materials, and theories for education. Be selective, but be open to what is possible.

4. *Take a few risks.* Maybe even tell your students that what you're about to do is something you're not quite sure about. Try those things that sound so good even though you're not

certain how they'll turn out. Most students believe in risk taking at a moderate level and will appreciate your sense of adventure and your desire for growth as an educator. Again, allow yourself not to be perfect, and give yourself permission to "bomb."

Some closing comments on student boredom. In all my years as a student, I never had a teacher who said anything like, "Tell me when you're bored." I have interviewed hundreds of students, and not one has ever had a teacher who said this either. I don't know why we are so reluctant to do it. Maybe we fear that we won't know what to do if our students tell us that they're bored. Maybe we think that we'll be abused. I'm not sure—but I do know that boredom is a killer. It kills student interest. It kills classroom enthusiasm. It kills us as teachers. Continuously bored students are cynical students. They have lost faith in learning and have given up their hope in what teachers have to offer. Their best bet is not to get excited or optimistic about what might happen in class because if they do, then the frustration of more boredom will only be more painful for them.

So I advocate something weird. Tell your students to tell you when they're bored. But put a reasonable time limit on it—after a few hours, or even a few days, if it makes sense. Some things take time to get started. And if they tell you that they're bored, see what *both* of you can do about it. It's their responsibility as well as ours. Learning is a mutual process. We can't do it all for students, and they can't do it all for us.

But don't let boredom continue. It's the cancer of education. We've grown accustomed to living with it, but its silent power overcomes. Unless we open ourselves up to it, we have no way to prevent or inhibit its destructive growth. And there is no sure cure. Students and teachers have to do their best to help themselves.

Chapter 5   Affect: Humanizing the Process

The affective factor pertains to the emotional experience—the feelings, concerns, values, and passions of the individual learner or her or his group—while learning. When we refer to the learning group, we usually describe their emotional state as the "climate" or classroom atmosphere.

My personal belief is that in any moment-to-moment learning experience, it is the emotional state of the student at that precise instance that governs her or his motivation to learn most significantly. The best check on any student's motivation at a given point in time is to simply ask the learner, "How do you feel about what you are doing right now?" In this manner, it is not "what" a student does but "how the student feels about what she/he is doing" that makes the difference regarding her or his involvement, perseverance, completion, or return to the learning activity. To make any lesson plan without attention to the student's emotional reaction to it is like planning for a dance without considering the music.

As Castillo has written, "The affective domain is the heart and soul of the learning experience, just as the cognitive domain is the thinking intellectual part. They are directly interrelated. The cognitive domain stimulates the affective domain, and, once the child is involved in affective experiences, new cognition arises." Teacher and student emotions give meaning and relevancy to learning. They "supercharge" life into the learning situation and provide energy for study and commitment.

Affect is an intrinsic motivator. It is "feeling while learning" that, when positive, sustains involvement and deepens interest in the subject matter or activity. If I study about local government, that is one thing—a possibly interesting topic. But if I study about "my" local government and can identify with my mayor, if I can consider my feelings about myself in an integrated school and my experience with the local police, that is something else—a real and vital topic.

It is important to note that if we avoid considering the emotions of our students in what we offer to them, we are denying not only their "humanness," but their integrity as well. Weinstein and Fantini clearly support this notion when they assert:

> Concerns, wants, interests, fears, anxieties, joys and other emotions and reactions to the world contain the seeds of "motivation." Dealing with the child's inner concerns constitutes recognition of, and respect for him. By validating his experiences and feelings, we tell the child, in essence, that he *does* know something. Probably this is the most important factor in linking relevant content with self-concept. For when the teacher indicates to the child in effect that the experience he brings with him has nothing to do with the "worthwhile" knowledge that the school intends to set before him, he is, without realizing it, telling the child in effect that *he* is worthless, for he *is* his experience.[2]

Students are "sensual beings." They respond to what their senses tell them, and they often do what seems pleasant at the moment. In this manner, feelings are motivating forces that naturally tell students what they need or want. From this perspective, there is no such thing as a "bad feeling." When a student is feeling sad, she/he probably has a sense of needing something for which she/he feels a sense of loss. Even anger, the most repressed feeling for both teachers and students, often emanates from a need for something that has been prevented, blocked, or frustrated. This is not to say that any behavior that results from feelings of fear, anger, etc., should be accepted by us; rather, unless students are aware of their feelings, and unless we as teachers can accept them, we cannot have effective motivation to learn from them. To deny what students really need and want by denying them any means to express their basic feelings puts learning in a context that is inhumane and intrinsically unrewarding.

I do not advocate some form of "affective supremacy" in today's classroom; I encourage a sense of harmony between affect and cognition so that they can influence motivation as an integrated force. Again, Weinstein and Fantini say it well:

> In urging that the teacher vigorously explore the affective domain we are not asserting its primacy over cognition or erecting a wall between cognition and affect. Indeed, cognitive learning is a natural way of becoming more capable of dealing with one's inner needs. The more analytic the person the more means he presumably has available for dealing with his feelings and concerns. Consequently, cognitive machinery should link inner needs to the environment and provide the organisms with means of coping with the requirements of the environment.[3]

In the classroom, more than anyone else, we as teachers influence our students' feelings daily. What we feel and how we express what we feel provide the model and stimulus for their feelings. This can easily become a cycle. If we feel bored and frustrated and if we express our boredom and frustration through sighing, complaining, and angry outbursts, we will, in most instances, receive restless and resentful behaviors from our students. Whereas, if we are genuinely enthusiastic and joyful in our teaching, it will be difficult for our students to escape our infectious manner, and their responses should be positive and pleasant. This is, of course, one of those "easier said than done" ideas. But a good place to begin is to identify our feelings in classroom situations and become more aware of what we do or do not share with our students.

Before you go on to the subfactors and strategies that follow, I want to encourage you to complete the exercise in Figure 11. It will give you a better sense of your affective feelings and expressiveness among your students. This is something to remain aware of when you consider adopting the strategies that are contained in this chapter.

Now we will move on to some subfactors of affect and their complementary strategies.

Feelings

Feelings are the everyday emotions that permeate living and learning for the individual student. Here, we mean primarily the

109

Figure 11[4]

1. Consider your classroom "teaching" behavior. Take a few moments to "see" yourself teaching a recent lesson. Reflect on how you interacted with your students, what you felt, and what you "showed" of what you felt. Consider this experience in the pattern of your everyday teaching. Try to get in touch with the emotions you do reveal to your students in your regular teaching.

2. After having taken some time for this reflection, look at the list below. These are emotions that most people have in different situations. Here, the emphasis is on becoming more aware of your feelings and expressing those feelings while teaching.

For each feeling, draw two X's and two lines. Let a dotted line represent how often you are *aware* of experiencing the feeling while teaching; let a solid line represent how often you *disclose* the feeling to your students.

There may be some variation between *awareness* and *disclosure*. For example, I may frequently be aware of feeling grateful to my students, but only sometimes express it to them, as shown below:

never   rarely   sometimes   frequently

grateful — — — — — — — — — — — — — — X *(awareness)*

————————————————————X *(disclosure)*

Whatever you experience, please be honest with yourself and accept your feelings as your own. Think of your feelings in terms of what is, rather than what should or shouldn't be, or what's good or bad.

FEELINGS	never	rarely	sometimes	frequently	FEELINGS	never	rarely	sometimes	frequently
stubborn					contented				
loving					sad				
weary					excited				
calm					sympathetic				
angry					fearful				
elated					bored				

FEELINGS	never	rarely	sometimes	frequently	FEELINGS	never	rarely	sometimes	frequently
jealous					proud				
disappointed					depressed				
grateful					satisfied				
embarrassed					shy				
cautious					lonely				
daring					tender				
confused					solemn				
uneasy					pleased				
sexy					guilty				
frustrated					appreciative				
surprised					happy				

3. When you have completed the exercise, consider which emotions you are aware of while teaching and how often you disclose them. Do they tend to be positive or negative? Which type do you disclose more easily? What does this mean?

4. Which emotions tend to be absent, and what might this mean?

5. When do you express your feelings? How is this done? How do students respond? How do you feel about their response?

Finally, consider what you have learned by doing this. From doing this exercise, *I learned* . . . *(feelings and thoughts about yourself and students).* This might mean I want to . . . *(intentions or desires).*

---

emotions that accompany *how* and *what* a student is learning. The two fundamental processes that allow feelings to become a vital and influential part of student motivation are *awareness* and *communication.*[5] As teachers, it is our awareness of our own, as well as student, emotions and of the ways that we communicate and accept them that facilitates their positive effect on student motivation.

Strategy 1: *When emotions are apparent, recognize and accept the student's feelings.* This is probably most helpful when the student's emotions tend to be negative, but it can be used with positive feelings as well. Students often become angry, frustrated, frightened, helpless, etc., when involved in daily class activities. To judge or negate these feelings is a sure way to increase hostility, resentment, or withdrawal and to cut off involvement and communication. Usually a simple statement like, "You seem ("feeling word") about ("facts")," can be enough to show our acceptance and give the student the necessary support to deal with her or his feelings. This allows the student to "own" her or his feelings and begin to use them to solve the problem. Some examples are as follows:

1. You give an assignment. A student slams the textbook shut and is staring at you tight-jawed and apparently sullen.

Avoid judgmental—"What kind of way is that for a person to act? Don't let me see that happen again." (You are totally authoritarian, with no chance for communication.)

Try acceptance—"You seem upset about the assignment I just gave. Let's talk about it." (You accept feelings without condoning them and allow for further communication.)

2. A student is agitated while working on math problems. You notice she/he is upset.

Avoid judgmental—"Don't be a baby. Just try your best." (This is a put down, even though the demand for achievement has been lessened.)

Try acceptance—"You seem frustrated by those problems. What's happening?" (You recognize the student's frustration and allow the student to voice her/his needs.)

3. A student is the first to finish a classroom exercise. She/he runs up to you obviously elated, and hands you the paper.

Avoid judgmental—"You certainly are smart to finish that quickly." (Although positive, it is an evaluation that makes you the judge.)

Try acceptance—"You seem quite happy about finishing so quickly." (You acknowledge the student's accomplishment and allow the student to feel her/his own personal sense of control.)

Strategy 2: *When there are strong feelings, possible misunderstandings, and/or conflicts between yourself and a student, paraphrase her or his message to continue communication and show understanding.* Paraphrasing is the skill of repeating the essence of what another person has just said in one's own words. It is helpful in potential conflict situations with students because (1) it demonstrates understanding to both parties; (2) it increases the chances for dialogue around the issue; and (3) it allows for a deeper appreciation of feelings. Some examples are:

1. You come to a student who seems confused about a seatwork assignment. You ask, "Would you like some help?"

The student responds, "I can take care of it myself. This stuff is just tricky. I'm having some trouble, but I'll do it."

You respond (paraphrase), "I get the message. You're saying you can do it yourself." (This shows your understanding and leaves responsibility with the student for requesting help.)

2. A student is late in bringing in a project. You ask, "When are you going to have it ready to hand in?"

The student responds, "Give me a chance. I know it's due but don't think I'm way behind. I just have a few more details to finish. Can't it wait a couple of days?"

You respond (paraphrase), "Then I understand you to say that you're almost done and that it will be ready in two more days. Is that right?" (This stops you from getting into a conflict with the student and decreases her/his defensiveness.)

Strategy 3: *When a student seems unmotivated, simply describe her/his behavior, and ask an open-ended question to facilitate understanding and resolution of the issue.* When a student is not learning or involved in learning activities, we often cut off communication about her/his feelings or anything else by attributing unfavorable motives, intentions, or character traits to the student. A behavior description clearly and specifically notes some of the overt behaviors of the student so that she/he can understand you without becoming defensive.

Some examples are:

1. "You haven't handed in an assignment in three days. What's happening?"

Not: "You're getting lazy. Where are the assignments for the last three days?"

2. "I haven't heard a comment from you in the last two discussion periods. I'm concerned."

Not: "You must be daydreaming again. You're not sharing in the discussions."

3. "This composition has five spelling errors and four grammatical mistakes. Was it proofread?"

Not: "This paper is a mess. You must not care about it."

Strategy 4: *Whenever a student's feelings seem relevant but are unstated or ambiguous, check your impression*[6] *of them to open communication and facilitate motivation.* This is similar to recognition and acceptance of feelings, but deals more with inference or tentative interpretation of a student's feelings based on words or behaviors of the student that do not directly reveal the student's emotions.

Many times a student who has a problem will not directly state her or his emotions. At such times our "checking out" of her or his emotions will give the student the freedom to deal with these feelings and resolve the issue.

Another common situation often occurs during discussion, when a student will make strong emotion-filled statements, but not directly reveal her/his feelings. At such times our tentative impression check about the student's feelings can free her/him to describe her/his *own* feelings and facilitate discussion. Some examples are as follows:

1. You ask a student if she/he wants to perform a certain task.

The student responds with a hesitant and low-voiced, "Yes."

You respond (impression check), "It sounds like you're not too sure." (The student can now affirm her/his Yes or reveal more uncertainty.)

2. You give an assignment to the class.

From the back of the room, a student asks in an angry and loud voice, "Does it have to be in by Friday?"

You respond (impression check), "I have the feeling that something about this assignment is disturbing to you." (You could simply have said, "Yes," but this would deny the real message and the feelings behind the student's question. Now, she/he can deal with them.)

3. A discussion is occurring among your students.

One student gives an opinion about the federal government. Another student immediately responds, "That's the biggest bunch of bunk I've ever heard!" There is a deadening silence among the class.

You respond (impression check), "You seem angry about the opposing opinion." (Now the student can deal with these feelings, if she/he chooses to do so. Scolding or reprimanding would have cut off feelings and discussion as well.)

Another possibility in all of the above situations is to ask the person, "What are you feeling now?" This may be too direct and cause defensiveness or withdrawal. However, if the feelings of students are there, and are influencing their behavior, a simple direct question of this nature can give permission for them to deal with their emotions and provide a better chance for communication and motivation. It is important to remember *not to force* such discussion and to leave the student "in charge" of her or his emotions.

Strategy 5: *Directly describe your feelings[7] to resolve problems with a student and to avoid continual anger and resentment.* In my opinion, continual teacher anger and resentment are the elements most destructive to classroom motivation. When I am angry, I am not humorous, enthusiastic, or empathetic. I am out to get someone—probably a student who is weaker and more vulnerable. I fear that there are too many of us who don't know what to do when we're angry. Personally, I was taught to withdraw or attack. Neither of these is very helpful to students or the classroom atmosphere. So if I hold my feelings in and deny their existence, the results are tension headaches, an upset stomach, or my own version of the "blahs."

What has helped me, and what I encourage you to consider, is that anger is a secondary emotion. Some other feeling has to occur first before I become angry. I feel "threatened," "frustrated," "abused," "guilty," "unable to maintain control," etc., before I feel angry. What I can do to help myself and my students is to get in touch with that *first* feeling and describe *what behavior* had what concrete effect that resulted in my feeling, and what I want to do about it. For example:

1. A student keeps talking while I'm talking.
Don't say, "Shut up!" (Dehumanizing command)
Say, "When you keep talking when I'm talking, I get distracted. I'm feeling frustrated now. Could you please stop?" (The student can now be responsible for her/his behavior and know what I'm feeling.)

2. A student knocks over a classroom display and stands there laughing about it.
Don't say, "Pick up that mess or you'll regret it." (Authoritarian threat)

115

Say, "When you knock over the display and do nothing constructive about it, I feel irritated. Could you pick it up?" (The student knows my feelings, is still treated respectfully, and can be responsible.)

3. A student calls me a bastard.

Don't say, "Leave the room. I'll take care of you later." (Implied threat and denial of my own as well as the student's feelings)

Say, "When you call me a bastard in front of the class, I feel insulted. Something's obviously wrong between us. I'd like to talk with you about it privately." (The class knows that I'm human and that I have feelings, but I accept the student and want to do something about the situation.)

This is hard to do. I admit that I have to continue to work at this daily and I am far from perfection. It's a "two-steps forward, one-step backward, two-steps forward" kind of progress. But when I don't do this, I usually find myself feeling resentful toward my students and then guilty about my resentment. That's like going from bad to worse. So if you identify with me, take a look at those books I referred to earlier in footnote 5 on page 111 as they relate to the topics of "description of own feeling," "I–messages," and "assertiveness."

Confluency

This subfactor is based on the extensive work of George I. Brown[8] and his colleagues. Essentially, confluency means to integrate whatever we teach with how the student feels *now* about the content and to establish a relationship between this content and the student's life. Therefore, all cognitive learning should be expanded and experienced through the student's personal experience in the "here and now." The student's awareness of self in relation to the subject matter is an important element for the teacher to constantly promote in daily instruction.

Strategy 1: *Have the student "live out"[9] the cognitive concepts presented by experiencing them in the classroom setting.* This allows the student to "vitalize" the learning by touching, seeing, hearing, smelling, and moving the concept in her/his own experience. For example, if we were teaching a unit on squares and circles to primary children, we might ask them to "become" a square and then a circle. We could ask them: "Where are your angles?" "How does it feel to be a square?" "How does it feel to be a circle?" "Which do you prefer?" "Can you move as either?" "How must you move your body to go from being a circle to a square?" Then we could ask students to name important square and circle shapes in their lives— i.e., clocks, houses, money, wheels, stoves, etc.

In a secondary situation, we might be teaching the concept of a phobia. We might ask students to imagine a phobia to which they might be susceptible. We might write down the class's list and compare and discuss them. Then we might select a few to role-play or fantasize about. Then we could ask how we might help someone to overcome her or his phobia. Again, the goal is to make the experience concrete and vital in the "here and now."

Strategy 2: *Have the student imagine and deal with learning experiences as they relate to her/his real life.* In this instance, we are seeking ways for students to relate what they learn to their current experiences. If we are studying a war, we might ask them how they would feel if they were "invaded" by an outside force. We might ask them to relate their experience around feelings of invasion of property, privacy, and rights. In talking about great military generals, we might ask whom they now see as powerful leaders and how these people compare to historic figures. We might discuss warfare or physical conflict and ask students to relate their own feelings on such matters to the experience of fighting soldiers. Perhaps, some of their relatives have been soldiers, and they will want to discuss this. We might also consider the role of the police in our society. The possibilities are immense for this subject, as well as for most, if we desire to "personalize" learning and increase its meaning through the acceptance of our students' daily lives as a motivational context for learning.

Strategy 3: *Use student concerns to organize content and to develop themes and teaching procedures.* According to Weinstein and Fantini,[10] a concern connotes an inner uneasiness for the student and is deeper and more persistent than a simple interest or feeling. They write:

> Interests usually are less anxiety-laden than concerns and they are more likely to be transitory. The term "concerns," as we are using it, connotes an inner uneasiness. Concerns are deeper and more persistent than interests. A person may have an interest (in, say, urban poverty) and yet not be concerned; on the other hand, his interests may give clues to his concerns. More-

over, as we have pointed out earlier, concerns go beyond "feelings" which do not necessarily arouse the frustration or anxiety associated with concerns . . . .

. . . Concerns may be positive of course, rooted in aspirations and desires that are seeking outlets. But all concerns are negative in the sense that they signify disequilibrium or incomplete satisfaction—the gap between reality and an ideal. The curriculum should deal with ways of helping students to work toward achieving their aspirations as well as toward overcoming fears and anxieties.[11]

We can learn about our students' concerns by empathetically listening to and observing what they say and write about their lives and their relations to the world. Since the frequency of their comments and clues will be an indicator of whether the problem is a fleeting feeling or a deep and persistent concern, our mental record of these events can guide us.

Let us say that we note that a positive self-image is a strong concern of our students. We can then establish some organizing ideas such as:

1. Parents and significant others help us to determine how we feel about ourselves.
2. Reaching important goals enhances our self-concept.
3. Feedback is an immediate way of knowing how well we are progressing toward our goals.
4. It is important to know what we use to measure our self-worth.

With these organizing ideas, we might choose to read *Catcher in the Rye* and outline and discuss—

1. Who the significant others in Holden's life were.
2. How his self-concept came from them.
3. What goals were important to him.
4. How he sought to achieve those goals.
5. How his self-concept compares with ours.
6. What his adventure means to us in knowing who we are.

This approach can lead to more discussion, a paper, library exploration, artistic symbols, etc. By making our students' concerns an influential theme in our daily lessons, we can nurture their self-actualization as well as motivation.

In all of the above strategies, teacher and student readiness is a necessary prerequisite before they are attempted. Some of these methods can be powerful, and if the student is not prepared, the strategy will have no meaning, and could even be harmful to the student. We may have to initially make a gradual progression or to take some time for the preparation of our students before attempting certain methods. Also, our own ability to handle our emotions as well as student feelings is something for us to consider. We must know how we respond to change, confusion, joy, anger, etc., so that we can be effective facilitators. The communication techniques stressed in the previous section, as well as our own personal security, are matters to carefully consider when incorporating these strategies in our daily teaching.

Valuing

Valuing means here a process that is commonly known as *values clarification*,[12] originally developed by Raths and based on the thinking of John Dewey. The process has three dimensions—choosing, prizing, and acting—with a total of seven subprocesses.

1. *Choosing:*

    a. *Choosing freely:* The person selects the value without coercion.

    b. *Choosing from alternatives:* By considering alternatives, the person has a greater probability to be "free" in her/his choice.

    c. *Choosing after considering the consequences:* The individual consciously attempts to predict what will happen if she/he chooses a particular value. This makes the choice more intelligent and less compulsive.

2. *Prizing:*

    a. *Prizing and cherishing:* The person respects the value and considers it an integral aspect of her or his existence.

    b. *Affirming:* The person will state the value publicly and, if necessary, share her or his respect for it when the occasion arises.

119

3. *Acting:*

    a. *Acting upon choices:* The value is apparent in the person's behavior and actions. The way the person spends her or his time reflects the cherished value.

    b. *Repeating:* The value is reflected in a consistent and repetitive pattern in the person's daily life. It is not inconsistent or unpredictable in the person's actions.

The advocates[13] of values clarification see it as an intervention to reduce value problems such as apathy, flightiness, overconformity, overdissention, and other behaviors indicative of lack of values or of value confusion. They claim that use of the valuing process helps individuals (and groups) to develop and clarify their values in such a way that they are more likely to (1) experience positive value in their own lives, and (2) act more constructively in the social context. I'm not so sure—but I *do* believe that values clarification in part or as a whole is a good method to facilitate student motivation because it asks students to relate to learning what they care about based on their personal awareness.

Strategy 1: *Use values clarification methods[14] and activities to facilitate learning.* Rather than attempt to superficially overview the field (a book would be necessary to do so), I want to illustrate the process of prizing by describing one of the most popular strategies called "Twenty Things You Love To Do."

The teacher asks the students to list the 20 things they most like to do. These can include anything from listening to the radio to building a house, and they can be important aspects of life or simple daily routines. After the lists are completed, the teacher suggests that the students place beside each activity certain symbols that will be self-revealing. For example:

1. Put a *D* next to each activity that costs more than a dollar to do each time.

2. Put a *P* next to each activity that either one or both of your parents enjoy doing as well.

3. Put an *S* next to each activity that you learned how to do in school.

4. Put an *A* next to each activity that you enjoy more if you do it alone.

5. Put a *C* next to each activity that you can do only in the city.

After this, the students are asked to reflect on their lists and symbols, and to complete the following sentence as many times as they can: "From doing this activity, I learned _____."

Some students may learn that what they like to do doesn't cost much. Some may learn that what they like to do is not something they learn in school. Some may learn that they enjoy their own company. There are many possibilities.

These lists and reactions can be shared in small groups and/or as a class. It should make for an interesting discussion about happiness and motivation.

There are some guidelines to follow in the use of these processes:

1. We accept different student values without being judgmental.

2. We don't permit students to "put down" others during the sharing of values.

3. We are willing to offer our own values without intimidation or self-righteousness.

4. We allow students not to participate, to "pass." The goal is to involve student values in learning and to nurture acceptance of different values.

Climate

Every classroom is a group, and every group has emotional and intellectual interplay among its members. These interrelationships have vibrations, feelings, and an expressive tone. Climate refers to the quality of the interrelationships among members in a learning group. When interactions are frustrating, hostile, and unaccepting, we have a group with a "negative classroom climate." When the characteristics of the interplay are supportive, friendly, and accepting, we have a "positive classroom climate." This can be seen and heard in how students move toward one another, how they address each other, how they solve problems, and how they relate to the teacher.

Students will not become spontaneous or expressive in their learning until they have learned that their peers and their teacher accept them. Those who do not feel accepted will feel alienated from the group as well as from academic learning. A rejecting classroom climate helps to create directionless and poorly motivated students who will supress their feelings and not abide by the academic norms of the classroom.

No matter how well we consider the individual attitude, needs, and feelings of each student, most learning takes place in a group, and unless the student feels accepted and respected by her or his peers, her or his motivation may be in jeopardy. (Remember your first year of teaching and how acceptance or rejection by your professional colleagues influenced your daily work?) As educational leaders in the classroom, we have the greatest responsibility to influence its atmosphere.

Yet, this is a tremendous task. Even the best learning groups, like the best families, have some degree of conflict. There are two inevitable issues for disagreement in any group that has work to accomplish (and learning often *is* work). The first involves reaching an effective balance between group goals and individual interests. Some students want to move ahead. Others want to stay behind. And some just want to go in different directions. Second, there is always the feelings of the group versus the feelings of the individual. Most students like a certain topic, but some don't. The majority of the class feels a need to discuss a problem, but a few feel it's unnecessary. These are not perfectly resolvable issues, and some degree of compromise or balance will have to be accomplished.

I say this not to discourage us, but to emphasize the need in every classroom to take time to deal with social–emotional concerns among the group. So give yourself permission to occasionally move away from the curriculum, without guilt, and to deal with what can't be denied or prevented. Schmuck and Schmuck[15] give us the research backing:

> One of the most important revelations of this research is that groups tend to alternate in a cyclical fashion between emphases on task and social–emotional concerns. When groups of students are asked to work together on classroom projects, it is realistic to expect that they too will spend nearly half of the available time dealing with emotional aspects of their interpersonal relationships. All groups, both student and adult, spend a great deal of time granting emotional support to their members.

122

Learning groups that do not solve their emotional problems also have difficulty in accomplishing academic learning tasks.[16]

Strategy 1: *Use Gibb's*[17] *supportive communication behaviors to facilitate a positive climate.* In his research, Gibb found that certain behaviors on the part of the communicator tended to produce a defensive climate in small groups. Such a climate is characterized by people who feel threatened and who tend to distort the messages of the sender. For each defensive-producing behavior, he also found a supportive communication behavior which operated on the same continuum but which was capable of facilitating a positive group atmosphere with trust and effective communication. We can foster a motivating group climate in our classrooms by using and modeling these positive characteristics while avoiding the defensive traits. There are six sets:

1. Avoid *judgmental and evaluative behavior* that puts students on guard and inhibits their reactions. Instead, use *descriptive speech* (see the strategies under the subfactor of "Feelings") that does not ask or imply that students should change their behavior or attitudes.

2. Avoid speech that is used to *control* students and implies that they are inadequate, ignorant, immature, or unwise. Instead, use a *problem orientation* with students that communicates a desire to collaborate in mutual problem solving (see the conflict resolution model—Strategy 4—below) and has no predetermined solution, attitude, or method to impose.

3. Avoid *unannounced strategies* or *hidden agendas* that make students feel used or victimized. Instead, use *direct and spontaneous communications* that are straightforward and honest. State your wants and needs clearly without manipulation. Both you and your students have a right to say, "No, I won't," as well as "Yes, I will."

4. Avoid *neutrality* or *noncaring behavior* toward students— e.g., "This is a democratic class. You can take it or leave it." Everyone wants to be perceived as a valued person, as someone of special worth. Instead, use communication that conveys *empathy* for student feelings (see the strategies under the subfactor of "Feelings") and respect for her/his worth.

123

According to Gibb, the combination of understanding and empathizing with a student's emotions with no accompanying effort to change her/him is supportive at a high level.

5. Avoid communication that implies superiority. Any time we behave as though we are "better" than our students, we are likely to allow them less status, power, and worth. They know this and resent us for it. Instead, use *equality behavior* that functionally accepts and respects student opinion; work with them to solve problems and plan activities.

6. Avoid *dogmatism* or *certainty* that implies there is only one answer, one way, or one method—ours. Not only is this too controlling of students, but it implies that they are inferior as well. Instead, be *exploratory and investigating* of issues and problems so that students can feel control over their lives and respect for their intellect in the quest for more information and learning.

Strategy 2: *Use a cooperative goal structure to maximize student involvement and sharing.* The way students relate to one another in working toward the accomplishment of academic goals appears to have a significant influence on their motivation.[18] A cooperative goal structure exists when students perceive that they can obtain their goal if, and only if, the other students with whom they are linked can obtain their goal. Two students writing a paper together and a group of students making a single project are examples of a cooperative goal structure.

The research in this area is important and indicates that—

1. Students will become more involved in instructional activities and tasks under cooperative rather than under competitive conditions.

2. Students prefer cooperatively structured learning situations over competitively structured ones.

3. Probable consequences of the use of continual competition are student anxiety and avoidance reactions, group fragmentation and hostility, and subversion of intrinsic motivation for learning. (All of this is a very nice and logical way of saying we should avoid continued competition in our classes if we want a positive climate with motivated students.)

The best types of instructional activities for a cooperative goal structure are problem solving, divergent thinking (creative tasks), and relatively ambiguous assignments in which students do the clarifying, decision making, and inquiring. Each student should be prepared through our instruction and facilitation to (1) see the learning goal as desirable, (2) expect the group to achieve the goal through sharing of ideas, and (3) count on mutual student support for risk taking and division of labor. In this approach, we are facilitators and advisers, but the students are themselves the major resource for assistance, support, and reinforcement.

Strategy 3: *Make group decisions by consensus.* Most of us attempt to be democratic in our teaching. When we approach situations, concerns, goals, and issues that affect all of our students, we usually ask their opinion and try to make a decision. Often there is a difference of opinion on certain matters among our students, so to reach resolution we "take a vote" with the majority determining the decision. Thus, we are fair and democratic. But with every *majority win*, there is a *minority loss* in the process. This leaves a few students or the minority "out of it," and often they feel rejected, resentful, and poorly motivated for the task at hand. To avoid this kind of possibility, I encourage consensus decision making in classroom matters.

Perfect consensus means that everyone agrees on what the decision should be. This is timely and difficult to achieve. I think it's worth it, but perfection is a demanding standard to continually sustain. So I suggest that lesser degrees of consensus might be appropriate, given the constraints of everyday classroom teaching. To continually work toward perfect consensus is a guideline that should enhance climate but not, because of our overly rigid application, defeat it.

When a decision is made by consensus, all students understand the decision and are prepared to support it. This means that all students can rephrase the decision to show that they comprehend it and that they've had a chance to tell how they feel about it. Those students with remaining doubts or disagreements are at least willing to publicly agree to give the decision a try for a period of time.

Discussion is best when students are seated in a circle with an atmosphere of support and acceptance. Differences of opinion are seen as ways to gather additional information, clarify issues, and seek better alternatives.

According to Johnson and Johnson,[19] the basic guidelines for consensual decision making are:

1. *Avoid blindly arguing for your own individual judgments.* Present your position as clearly and logically as possible, but listen to other members' reactions and consider them carefully before you press your point.

2. *Avoid changing your mind* only *to reach agreement and to avoid conflict.* Support only solutions with which you are at least somewhat able to agree. Yield only to positions that have objective and logically sound foundations.

3. *Avoid "conflict-reducing" procedures*—e.g., taking a majority vote, tossing a coin, averaging, or bargaining in reaching decisions.

4. *Seek out differences of opinion.* They are natural and expected. Disagreements can help the group's decision because they present a wide range of information and opinions, thereby creating a better chance for the group to hit upon more adequate solutions.

5. *Do not assume that someone must win and someone must lose when discussion reaches a stalemate.* Instead, look for the next most acceptable alternative for all members.

6. *Discuss underlying assumptions, listen carefully to one another, and encourage the participation of all members.*[20]

Some practice of this method with students through role playing and/or exercises may be helpful before its use with real and emotionally laden issues. This is a skill, and good intentions are not enough to make it work.

Strategy 4: *For problems with a student or group of students, use Gordon's[21] Conflict Resolution Model.* This is similar to the consensus decision-making strategy outlined above, but it focuses more strongly on conflict (teacher needs interfering with student needs or vice versa) and individual needs. All of the interpersonal skills outlined as strategies with the subfactor of "Feelings" are necessary for successful implementation of this method.

Probably one of the "moments of truth" in any classroom is when a student feels justified in meeting her or his individual needs but finds herself or himself in conflict with the group and/or teacher. If we attempt to authoritatively "force" the student to submit, we will have on our hands, at best, an obedient but resentful student or, at worst, a rebellious and hostile student. This not only "kills" the student's motivation but also may negatively affect the motivation of her or his peers who are observing the situation. Gordon's method is a "win–win" approach which respects the rights of both parties. His six steps are:

1. *Defining the problem*—Both individuals have a turn to state what they think the problem is and to convey any feelings they might have about it until agreement on a definition of the problem is reached. The problem is stated in terms of needs and wants, and not solutions.

EXAMPLE: Teacher—"I want you to do these 20 math problems, but you don't think it's necessary."

Student—"That's right, you think I need the practice, but I believe I don't. I don't want to do what's unnecessary and boring."

Teacher—"Okay, let's see if we can resolve this."

2. *Generate possible alternatives or solutions*—The teacher and student brainstorm and come up with possible solutions and alternatives (be creative). There is no evaluation or criticism at this point. If things bog down, the problem is stated and re-examined.

EXAMPLE: a. Do all of the math problems.

   b. Do none of the math problems.

   c. Do half of the math problems.

   d. Go on to the next assignment.

   e. Just hand in the answers.

   f. If the first five math problems are done correctly, do no more.

   g. Do a random selection of four math problems, and if all are done correctly, go on to the next assignment.

3. *Evaluate the possible solutions and alternatives*—Estimate and critique the possible alternatives and solutions for meeting each person's needs or wants. Check them for flaws, reasoning, fairness, implementation, and appeal. Be honest and direct.

EXAMPLE: a. Do all of the math problems. (Student—"I can't accept this one.")

      b. Do none of the math problems. (Teacher—"Well, I can't accept this either.")

      c. Do half of the math problems. (Teacher—"Maybe." Student—"It still doesn't seem fair to me.")

      d. Go on to the next assignment. (Teacher—"No, I have to have some assurance you can do these problems well.")

      e. Just hand in the answers. (Teacher—"That's less work and I'd know if you could do it." Student—"It still doesn't seem fair.")

      f. If the first five math problems are done correctly, do no more. (Student—"I like this one." Teacher—"But the first five are the easiest problems.")

      g. Do a random selection of four math problems, and if all are done correctly, go on to the next assignment. (Student—"Seems fair." Teacher—"Well, that's a possibility.")

4. *Decide on a mutually acceptable solution*—Select the solution that appears most agreeable to both parties. State the solution or write it down to make certain that everyone understands and accepts it.

EXAMPLE: Teacher—"Well, it seems that *doing the random selection of four problems and proceeding on to the next assignment if all of those are done correctly* is the solution we can both live with."

Student—"Yes, I'll go along with that."

5. *Implementing the solution*—This is essentially who does what by what time. Be specific, and, where necessary, use a deadline to avoid delay or confusion.

EXAMPLE: Teacher—"I'll randomly choose the problems and give them to you right now."

Student—"Okay, let's get started."

6. *Evaluate the solution*—Because of unforeseen difficulties or changes in the person or situation, the solution may need revision and/or another problem-solving attempt. Therefore, the contract is

always open-ended. Also, it may be wise to discuss the solution for future learning.

EXAMPLE: Student—"I see that all four problems are correctly answered. I knew I could do this stuff."

Teacher—"I have to admit that you were right. However, I did notice that you did those problems awfully carefully and very slowly."

Student—"That's because my pencil was dull and my arm was hurting me."

Teacher—"Sure, I know. Why don't you try the next assignment before your other arm starts hurting you?"

Student—"Okay."

Conflict resolution is not as easy or as simple as it appears in the previous example. But my experience is that it is extremely effective (especially with adolescents) and can turn a potentially explosive conflict into a creative challenge with positive payoff for students and teacher.

Strategy 5: *Use "climate surveys" to diagnose your classroom atmosphere.* These can be used to improve as well as affirm teaching practices and communication skills. Such feedback is important in the initial stages of group cohesion to increase our awareness of the student's viewpoint. Maintenance checks are also advisable to prevent the development of interpersonal relationship problems and to continue constructive motivation processes. One possible approach is to list a continuum of opposite descriptive terms on which students can mark to indicate their feelings about the classroom climate. (I encourage a sharing of the results of such a survey during a class meeting in order to discuss and clarify understanding as well as any necessary decision making that might result from the survey.)

The survey in Figure 12 is one of many possible instruments to gain student feedback. Change of or addition to the terms used is at the teacher's discretion, depending on the particular grade level and situation. An anonymous response by students is probably most desirable.

Strategy 6: *Use self-diagnostic questioning procedures to reflect upon how your behavior influences the classroom atmosphere.* Continued vitality and affirmation as a teacher are dependent on our own

129

Figure 12

Please mark the appropriate space on the following continuum that best describes our classroom climate as you experience it.

The atmosphere in this classroom for me:

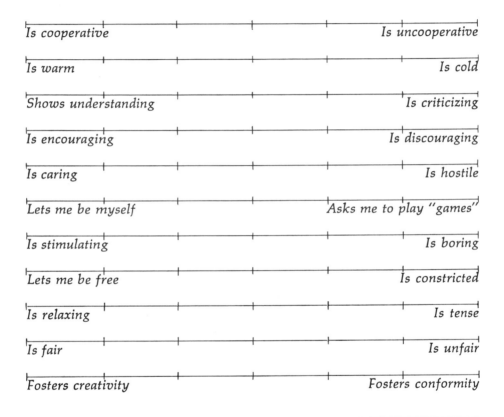

Is cooperative   _Is uncooperative_

Is warm   _Is cold_

Shows understanding   _Is criticizing_

Is encouraging   _Is discouraging_

Is caring   _Is hostile_

Lets me be myself   _Asks me to play "games"_

Is stimulating   _Is boring_

Lets me be free   _Is constricted_

Is relaxing   _Is tense_

Is fair   _Is unfair_

Fosters creativity   _Fosters conformity_

self-awareness. Because the facilitation of groups is such a demanding and complex process, some form of programmatic guideline for self-diagnosis of our group leadership behavior can be immensely helpful. Johnson and Johnson provide a series of questions and ratings that can aid our self-understanding. The list of questions in Figure 13 can be used in conjunction with the "climate survey" in Strategy 5 to make comparisons of what we think we do and of how well our class may perceive the results of our actions. This kind of mutual feedback (our self-perception and the students' climate evaluations) can help us to pinpoint our inconsistencies or flaws that may need further refinement or improvement.

This self-awareness inventory of group behavior can also be given to students to allow them to check their behavior and to reflect on what they do in class and what they might want to affirm, change, or improve.

These questions focus upon several aspects of increasing a positive classroom atmosphere. The first question deals with a general attempt to keep group cohesion high. Questions 2 and 3 pertain to the expression of ideas and feelings and the support for students who express ideas and feelings: Such personal participation is essential for cohesiveness and for the development of trust. Questions 4 and 8 also focus upon support for and liking of students. Question 5 refers to including students, and Question 6 takes up our willingness to be influenced by students. Questions 7 and 9 center on the acceptance of individuality within the class. By adding all of our answers, we can arrive at a total group behavior score. This can be used as a baseline measure to improve (raise) as the academic year continues. Classroom discussion of the results of this self-diagnosis may be helpful to continuing and improving a positive climate.

I would like to conclude this chapter with some comments about teacher vulnerability. I have often asked myself why it is so difficult for me to directly express my feelings in class or, better yet, just to "be myself" among students. In large part, I believe this resistance is due to my fear of student rejection and judgment. What if I were myself and they laughed at me or ridiculed me? This might happen, and I know I would be hurt and feel considerable pain. So if I play a role and avoid being myself and being direct about how I feel, I can reduce the threat of student ridicule and more easily feel superior and in control. I excuse this behavior by telling myself, "I know who I am and that's my business. I don't have to reveal myself." True. But when I maintain a role and remain an image, my students are encouraged by my "modeling" to do the same. We may get along but without real contact. There's less pain—but there's also less joy in teaching.

So when the human relations "types" come around and encourage me to "be myself," "act natural," and "let it all hang out," I respond, "That's easy for you, but you don't live with my students. They can

Figure 13[22]

Consider your classroom leadership behavior and answer each question as honestly as possible:

1. I try to make sure that everyone enjoys being a member of the class.

NEVER 1 : 2 : 3 : 4 : 5 : 6 : 7 : 8 : 9 ALWAYS

2. I disclose my ideas, feelings, and reactions to what is currently taking place within the class.

NEVER 1 : 2 : 3 : 4 : 5 : 6 : 7 : 8 : 9 ALWAYS

3. I express acceptance and support when students disclose their ideas, feelings, and reactions to what is currently taking place in the class.

NEVER 1 : 2 : 3 : 4 : 5 : 6 : 7 : 8 : 9 ALWAYS

4. I try to make all students feel valued and appreciated.

NEVER 1 : 2 : 3 : 4 : 5 : 6 : 7 : 8 : 9 ALWAYS

5. I try to include all available students in class activities.

NEVER 1 : 2 : 3 : 4 : 5 : 6 : 7 : 8 : 9 ALWAYS

6. I am influenced by other class members (students).

NEVER 1 : 2 : 3 : 4 : 5 : 6 : 7 : 8 : 9 ALWAYS

7. I take risks in expressing new ideas and current feelings.

NEVER 1 : 2 : 3 : 4 : 5 : 6 : 7 : 8 : 9 ALWAYS

8. I express liking, affection, and concern for all students.

NEVER 1 : 2 : 3 : 4 : 5 : 6 : 7 : 8 : 9 ALWAYS

9. I encourage class norms that support individuality and personal expression.

NEVER 1 : 2 : 3 : 4 : 5 : 6 : 7 : 8 : 9 ALWAYS

be nasty!" Again, true. There is no getting away from the risk. I realize this and encourage you to fully learn the strategies in this section and to comprehensively involve yourself in some of the recommended books and their related training. And with this, to gradually attempt the suggestions that have been outlined, to allow yourself time, and to permit yourself to be vulnerable, but not foolishly. Like a plant, growth only occurs with healthy exposure to the environment, and the plant grows best with careful nurturance.

| Chapter 6 | **Competence: Effectiveness with Responsibility** |

According to R. W. White[1] the desire to gain competence over one's environment is a powerful human motivation. In essence, this competence is experienced through the "organism's capability to interact effectively with its environment."[2] White[3] sees people not merely as the result of the influence of their experiences but also as active and reasoning beings who can shape the course of their development. Competence is used as a term to describe a person's ability to take the initiative and capably act upon her/his environment rather than remaining passive and allowing the environment to control and determine her/his behavior. People want to do more than to survive or exist. They want to effectively live and master what is important to their daily being.

For White, learning and achievement are intrinsically satisfying and rewarding in and of themselves: ". . . intrinsic satisfaction comes from expending effort and producing consequences."[4] Thus, when a student learns and feels an actual sense of progress and real accomplishment, there is significant motivation for further effort and learning in a similar direction. In general learning situations, a sense of competence occurs along two dimensions. The first is an awareness of mastery: the realization by the person that a specified degree of knowledge or level of performance has been attained that is acceptable by personal and/or social standards. The second is a sense of self-confidence: the self-perception that one is able and adept, whatever the task. For students, the mastery component results in statements such as, "I am doing it," or better yet, "I am doing it proficiently and effectively." The self-confidence is contained in statements such as, "I know I could do it," or, "I can do it." These internal messages complement each other and facilitate motivation for learning as the process continues.

In Nardine's[5] view, the relationship between mastery and self-confidence is a spiral one, and student growth requires that both be present.

> Knowledge and mastery ideally lead to development of confidence in one's skill and ability, and confidence supports the efforts to master new skills, the achievement of which in turn buttresses confidence. Thus self-confidence is a *sine qua non* of competence growth as it provides the basis for taking risks and for expanding one's skills into new areas.
> . . . The role of the school then must be to foster both cognitive growth and an appropriate sense of confidence in one's efficiency and ability to learn new skills if we are to graduate competent individuals who will initiate their own further or ongoing education.[6]

A construct similar and related to the concept of competence is the need to achieve. Achievement motivation, in general, is one's functional display of a concern for excellence in work that one values, and, in a sense, it is also a desire for competence over a body of subject matter, a specific skill, or a designated task. Achievement motivation involves the process of planning and striving for excellence and progress; doing things better, faster, more efficiently; doing something unique; or, in general, competing with a personal or social standard. Investigators[7] have found that a person with high achievement motivation is an individual who is self-confident, is a moderate risk-taker, wants immediate concrete feedback on her/his efforts, knows how to utilize her/his environment, and can tolerate delayed gratification for personal goals. It appears that students who have a high need to achieve usually do well in academic performance.

The theories of competence and achievement motivation are obvious in the programs and research of deCharms[8] and his colleagues who approach motivation with the concept of "personal causation." Their fundamental assumption about motivation is: "Man's primary motivational propensity is to be effective in producing changes in his environment. Man strives to be a causal agent, to be the primary locus of causation for, or the 'Origin of' his behavior, he strives for personal causation."[9]

In their significant and successful classroom motivation development project, students were told that Origins are persons who—

1. Take *personal responsibility.*
2. *Prepare* their work carefully.
3. *Plan* their lives to help reach their goals.
4. *Practice* their skills.
5. *Persist* in their work.
6. *Have patience,* for they know that some goals take time to reach.
7. *Perform,* for they know that they have to do things in order to reach their goals.
8. Check their *progress*—i.e., use feedback.
9. Move toward *perfecting* their skills, paying special attention to improvement.[10]

Personal causation training differs from achievement motivation programs by emphasizing assumptions and related strategies that enhance the student's internal ability to become committed to her or his learning by responsibly pursuing academic goals that have personal meaning. Achievement motivation appears to rely more on giving equal weight to striving for personal standards and standards set by others. In personal causation training, students are encouraged to use an internal choice of purpose followed by internal personal responsibility, not external accountability. deCharms warns, "Too often in the educational setting, at least, standards, excellence and efficiency are all imposed by superiors and hence reduce rather than enhance feelings of personal causation."[11]

Whatever their differences, there is no doubt that all of the theories and research cited above support personal self-confidence and effectiveness in learning as profound influences on continued student motivation.[12]

The rest of this chapter is devoted to accounting and elaborating on how student self-confidence and effectiveness in learning can be facilitated at the *end* of an academic task or experience. The student's sense of competence at the end of any learning task is a dominant factor in continued motivation for the task and the initiation of any similar activities.

I see this in what I call the "hinge head phenomenon." This seems especially apparent in passive learning situations where students must listen to us deliver information or demonstrate something. They politely listen and *nod* their heads, seemingly involved and attentive, but if they have not mastered the material or cannot see any value in the learning for their own effectiveness, when they can leave the situation, they are often *shaking* their heads and discounting the value of the experience.

Means and ways to facilitate student competence at the beginning and during a learning task can be found in the strategies for the subfactors of "Attitude Toward the Self," "Expectancy for Success," "Esteem Needs," "The Need for Self-Actualization," and "Interest and Involvement." What is emphasized in the following subfactors and strategies is what can be done when a learning task or activity is in the process of ending.

Awareness of Progress and Mastery

It is important to note that mastery is used here to mean the student's sense of effectiveness in dealing with personal learning; functionally, this refers to how the student perceives how proficiently she/he is personally causing and affecting learning in a chosen task that has personal meaning and value. A student's awareness of personal mastery grows out of continual knowledge of feedback from the learning environment that demonstrates the results that the student has produced. The student's accurate assessment of the feedback becomes the basis for her or his motivation to continue or retreat from further challenges in this learning.

Strategy 1: *Provide consistent feedback regarding mastery of learning.* Functionally, feedback is student awareness of a consequence that has occurred as a result of a personal response that has been completed. To be *immediate*, the awareness of the consequence must occur before another response is made. Immediate feedback is probably the best kind to facilitate motivation, but it is also very difficult for us to continually ensure. While psychomotor tasks such as riding a bicycle or jumping a hurdle give immediate feedback by their very nature, many forms of cognitive and affective learning do not. Programmed texts, teaching machines, computer-assisted instruction, and chemically processed materials, when high in quality, can give immediate feedback and should be examined for potential use. However, most of us will probably have to be innovative and develop our own techniques. Some possible suggestions follow. Their effectiveness is dependent on how clearly and how immediately they can provide helpful feedback that enhances the student's sense of progress and mastery in learning.

1. *Use a tutoring approach.* The tutor can be yourself, a teacher aide, a community volunteer, a parent, or another student. The process can be on an individual or a small group basis, with short meetings to give the feedback necessary. Advanced students can assist the less advanced members of the class, but be careful not to abuse this device by impeding the creativity and possible other learning outcomes for the more able students. Anyone who serves as a tutor should be carefully monitored to assure that the tutor is able to sensitively relate to those students whom she/he is assisting.

2. *Provide answer sheets, study guides, evaluation criteria, and models by which students can evaluate their own progress.* This can take the form of individual self-guidance, small group activities with "feedback leaders" who facilitate the process, or discussions in which divergent products are considered in a dialogue analogous to a group of movie directors who might be comparing their films at a seminar.

3. *Use tests and exams, whether they be written, oral, or performance, but primarily in a* diagnostic and formative *sense.* This means that they are *nongraded* and are used essentially as part of the teaching–learning process to give continuous feedback, to assess strengths and weaknesses in student learning, to diagnose areas of learning for progress and improvement, and to enhance instruction.

Although there is no "law of nature" that says, "All exams must be graded," most of us seem to feel compelled to grade tests. This makes tests and exams "anxiety ridden" for students, discourages learning for the sake of interest and enjoyment, encourages cramming and learning for the sake of passing an exam (which has the poorest transfer and retention rate), and distorts knowledge by confining it to what can be measured by a test or examination. This compulsion to grade every test is probably one of the most significant contributors to the "death of motivation" among students for learning and school. In this manner, one of the primary means by which they can get useful feedback is a "painful experience" from which they learn that mistakes are only counted against them and that the learning that "pays" is to figure out what the teacher will put on the exam and feed it back. In my opinion, it is the "rare" student who can endure this ritual on a weekly and a monthly basis for 12 years and emerge from high school eager to learn.

My experience is that students enjoy and relish taking exams and quizzes when these assessments are—

a. Related to goals and objectives that students understand and want to achieve.

b. Reflective of progress in learning.

c. Diagnostic and point out ways to improve learning without penalizing the student.

d. Expected.

e. Used for discussion and further understanding.

f. Returned quickly.

g. Permeated with teacher comments that are informative and supportive.

h. Used to encourage new challenges in learning.

4. *Use a variety of feedback procedures.*[13] Although the tutoring model, self-evaluation processes, and examinations tend to be the most common and efficient, many other possibilities exist. Some are:

a. Observation feedback.

b. Anecdotal records.

c. Role playing.

d. Any form of constructive commentary on journals, papers, models, projects, and demonstrations.

e. Group dialogue and discussions.

f. Dramatization.

g. Experiments.

h. Progress charts, records, and models.

Strategy 2: *Use constructive criticism.* Feedback often is criticism.

It points out errors, misplanning, faulty assumptions, unclear goals, unreasonable estimates, and weaknesses. But if it's honest and direct, affirms the positive, and clearly shows the way to improvement without manipulation or intimidation, it can be constructive. This translates into:

1. *Emphasizing what a student has accomplished*—not just what remains to be done.

For example—"You've almost finished your project. I've noticed that your writing is creative and that the designs are very imaginative. It seems that you're having some trouble coming up with an ending. Things just aren't fitting together. Would you like to talk about it?"

Not—"I see you haven't finished yet. I'd better help you."

2. *Emphasizing what's right and pointing out what's wrong, with ways to improve as well.*

For example—"You've done 16 out of 20 problems correctly. That's great. Let's look at the other four to see what can be done."

Not—"You had four problems wrong. Let's take a look at your mistakes."

3. *Helping the student to see things in the context of overall progress and not the momentary failure.*

For example—"This science unit has really been tough for you. Your exam indicates that 80% of the concepts are still unclear to your understanding. I hope you keep in mind that you've already progressed through four units, and although this one seems rough, that's a pretty good indication that you can do it. Let's go over the material."

Strategy 3: *Facilitate successful completion of the agreed-upon learning task.* One of the surest ways for us to know that we are competent is "to finish what we *wanted* to start": to reach that goal, to make that mark, to complete that book—in general, to release that sigh of satisfaction, knowing that we've done what we've intended to do. This is a tremendously self-enhancing moment. Students can experience it often with our facilitation. We may have to give them more time. We may have to individualize. We may have to help them to set shorter and more achievable goals. But we are deadening their motivation if we interrupt and take away their opportunities for successful completion in learning.

In essence, this means avoiding fixed or standard academic goals in which all students are expected to achieve at the same rate with the same instruction and materials. Benjamin Bloom[14] leaves no doubt about the motivational destructiveness of standardized curricula that do not allow for individual learning rates but rather support a normal distribution of student performance.

This set of expectations, which fixes the academic goals of teachers and students, is the most wasteful and destructive aspect of the present educational system. It reduces the aspirations of both teachers and students; it reduces motivation for learning in students; and it systematically destroys the ego and self-concept of a sizable group of students who are legally required to attend school for 10 to 12 years under conditions which are frustrating and humiliating year after year.[15]

Strategy 4: *Help the learner to realize how to operationalize in daily living what has been learned.* This may be done with the individual student or the entire class. It is one of the best ways to conclude a learning activity, to promote transfer to other learning, and to firmly demonstrate how the new learning can help the student to increase personal effectiveness. It can be done through application questioning, role playing, simulation, and discussion as well as the other active learning processes.

For example:

1. *Application*—"You've just finished our geology unit. How can you use what you've learned when you visit some of the local parks?"

   "I know you like to garden. How does this math lesson relate to your hobby?"

   "Creative writing is something you really enjoy. What does this project on mysticism mean for that interest?"

2. *Role playing*—"Class, let's put these communication skills to task by role playing some situations in which we experience daily conflict."

   "Class, having studied the judicial system in this country, why don't we find some current cases in the local papers and have our own mock trials."

   "Folks, the three of you have been working on this project (famous scientists of the twentieth century) for a month now. What if each of you chooses one scientist to role play, and the class can interview you as a panel to learn about you and your work?"

3. *Simulation*—"Your drafting skills are terrific; let's imagine that I'm designing a room and that I will use you as the architect–consultant."

   "Okay, these map skills seem to be well learned. Let's try making our own maps to places of personal interest."

   "You've really put quite a project together on nutrition and dieting. What if a few of us listed our 10 most favorite foods and asked you to make a balanced weekly diet from those lists for us?"

4. *Discussion*—"Let's talk about some ways to use what we're learning today in our daily lives."

   "What kind of plans could we make for government spending based on the information we just received?"

   "How do you see this learning as making you a more effective person?"

In all of these suggestions, the idea is to allow students, through active processes, to put to use and affirm their enhanced personal effectiveness that has been gained through their learning experiences. This confirms not only that they, indeed, know something, but also that their learning has life and meaning in areas they value and for which their personal mastery is an actual asset.

Responsibility

Essentially, this means that the student is aware at the completion of learning that she/he has "personally caused" her or his own learning. Functionally, this means that the student is alert to and can comprehend that she/he has—

1. Been learning with a sense of purpose or personal motivation.

2. Planned and organized for the final outcome.

3. Used her or his own concrete actions to attain learning.

4. Been responsible for the success or failure of her or his actions.

5. Made a series of choices in reaching the learning outcome.

6. Related interdependently with others to achieve learning.

When students realize that they have been "responsible" as outlined above, they can affirm their sense of effectiveness and build self-confidence for future learning tasks. This does not mean that they are independent or infallible, but that beyond anyone else, it is they who control their lives and make the largest difference in affecting what they learn and how well they learn it. We, as well as they, know learning has occurred with the help of teachers, materials, and instructional processes in cooperation with other students. None of this is denied. However, my emphasis here is on the matter of degree—students who are motivated can continue their motivation to learn when they realistically know that they play the largest part in determining their learning through their own effective choice and involvement. For younger children, this may be much more difficult to comprehend, but it is certainly worthwhile to pursue to that degree that it is possible.

Strategy 1: *Acknowledge and affirm the student's responsibility in completing the learning task.* The degree to which this is done is dependent on time, the magnitude of the task, other student needs, etc. It can be done individually, with small groups, or with the entire class. Again, we have to use our best judgment. Some guidelines are as follows:

1. *Celebrate.* Festivals and merrymaking have for centuries been the joyous social means to acknowledge the endings of seasons, harvests, religious periods, etc. There is no valid reason to avoid this in learning. Savor with the students their moment of triumph and accomplishment. This can be a pleasurable discussion, a party, a round of applause, sitting back and reliving the experience through "remember when" statements, or mild congratulations. But let the moment linger and enjoy it together. It is a happy occasion—not to be taken for granted.

2. *Affirm the strengths of each student in accomplishing the task.* This can be done by you for them, by them for themselves, or by all of you for each other. Not only does this build class morale, but also it allows students to realize and appreciate what is good about themselves and others. This is a process of giving, receiving, and sharing. This is the time to—

a. *Recognize talents*—"There's no doubt that you know your fractions." "I admire your creative abilities in making this."

b. *Acknowledge perseverance*—"You really hung in there." "There was no doubt you knew what you wanted and were going to do it."

c. *Acknowledge planning*—"Your organization was efficient." "That goal-setting scheme really worked."

d. *Point out significant actions*—"When you helped Tom, we made a real breakthrough." "Doing those last five problems was the hardest, but after that, I think your confidence began to emerge."

e. *Appreciate choice*—"When you selected that topic, I knew things would get exciting." "The methods you chose seemed to work best for you."

f. *Acknowledge cooperation*—"I admire the way you cooperated to get this done." "Working together was the most fun."

Whichever method you employ, sincerity and genuineness are absolutely necessary for this procedure to be effective. Some students will be uncomfortable in receiving recognition or acknowledgment. In those instances, a private talk or a self-awareness guideline which incorporates the above factors may be more appropriate. (The strategies found under the subfactors of "Feelings" and "Climate" are helpful to this process.)

3. *Ask the student for opinions as to how and what were the critical processes that helped her/him to achieve this learning.* Simple and direct questions such as the following can broaden their awareness of what they did to "make learning happen."

a. What did you do that made this task achievable?

b. How were you the prime reason for your own learning?

c. What do you think was most significant in accomplishing this task?

d. Which choices did you make that led to this accomplishment?

e. What have you learned about yourself from doing this?

Any questions directed to the various aspects of student responsibility for learning can help students to focus their attention on their effectiveness in bringing about their own learning.

Strategy 2: *Use a competence checklist for student self-rating.* This can be done with middle elementary and older students. The main purpose is to allow students to continually survey their own competence, periodically and/or after significant learning tasks. In this manner, they can work to enhance their sense of personal effectiveness by consistently being aware of their progress in the various aspects of responsible learning. These checklists can be used for conferences with students as well as for setting personal goals throughout the year. The items found in the checklist in Figure 14 are drawn mainly from achievement motivation and personal causation research. The list is not meant to be final, and you are welcome to add to or to improvise on its structure. Each item can serve as a personal incentive to help students to continue to self-determine their own learning.

Strategy 3: *Acknowledge the risk taking and challenge involved in the learning accomplishment.* Risk taking is a deliberate personal encounter with the unknown.[16] A challenge is the acceptance of a risk because it involves doing something in which the outcome of success is uncertain. The essence of any challenge is that we might fail at what we want to do. The greater the challenge, the greater the probability of failure. This is where courage and learning meet.

Students who choose a challenging learning goal are risking failure. When this is done with reflection and moderation, it can build student self-confidence and allow students to experience the merit of their abilities and effort. In such instances, nonachievement of the goal can be a lesson in reality testing that encourages self-appraisal and further decision making.

When there is success, there is good reason for jubilation and self-affirmation. When there is failure, the related issues can be expressed through three questions:

1. What has been learned from attempting to achieve the goal?

2. Does the goal remain worthwhile?

3. Is it reasonable to continue to strive for the goal?

In either success or failure, we can acknowledge what the student

Figure 14

Directions:

Put an X under Column 1 if you almost always have to have help to perform the behavior.

Put an X under Column 2 if you usually have to have help to perform the behavior.

Put an X under Column 3 if you sometimes have to have help to perform the behavior.

Put an X under Column 4 if you usually perform the behavior through your own effort.

Put an X under Column 5 if you almost always perform the behavior through your own effort.

	1	2	3	4	5
1. I choose learning goals that I want to accomplish.					
2. I plan how to achieve the learning goals that I have chosen.					
3. I continue to work toward the learning goals that I have chosen.					
4. I complete the learning goals that I have chosen.					
5. I accept the consequences of my learning.					
6. I am cooperative with other students when I learn.					
7. I evaluate the results of my learning.					
8. I practice those skills that are necessary to my learning until I am satisfied with them.					

Figure 14

		1	2	3	4	5
9.	I have patience to reach the learning goals that take time to achieve.					
10.	I check my own progress in learning.					
11.	I use my values to make choices for learning where alternatives are available.					
12.	I have personal standards by which I judge the quality of my learning.					
13.	I creatively use my environment to solve problems when I am learning.					
14.	I take moderate risks when learning to stretch my abilities and talents.					
15.	I choose challenging learning goals.					
16.	If I make mistakes, I try to correct them.					
17.	I work at my own speed.					
18.	I decide how to use extra time.					
19.	I ask questions when I do not understand.					
20.	I express my opinions in group tasks.					

has risked and how the acceptance of and the striving toward a challenge have benefited the student. This is best done through discussion with the student. Risk taking and accepting the challenge of learning which is personally valued, when habitual, become courage— the courage to think, the courage to question, the courage to create.

These are not inborn qualities. They are cultivated and evolve. We can help them to emerge by reflecting to students where they occur and by acknowledging their merit in our daily teacher–student relations.

Competition

It seems to me that some discussion of competition might serve as an apt conclusion to this chapter. Since I have not thoroughly dealt with competition, you may wonder why. Many people regard competition as a prime motivational force in academics. Competing is seen as a means to demonstrate mastery and effectiveness. In fact, some would even say that competition derives its meaning from competence, just as it follows the latter word in most household dictionaries. But this is not so. To compete is to contest, to enter into a rivalry for some external recognition or reward, with the final goal being to win. To be competent is to do something in a manner that is considered effective by one's personal standards. The goal is excellence, but no rival, contest, or victory is necessary. In fact, as I will suggest, competition often subverts competence as well as excellence.

It is currently in vogue to depreciate competition. And though I don't like jumping on bandwagons, I feel that the arguments against competitive methods of learning are so valid that I must confirm them. However, I see the desire for competition as a value, and values are difficult to objectively refute. They can only be subjectively argued against with facts, figures, opinions, and research. But emotions sustain values, and every day we choose to compete rather than to cooperate. We prize and cherish our competition with awards and public recognition. And we repeatedly continue to enter competitive activities for the extrinsic rewards they offer.

So I will give you my 10 reasons[17] why we are unwise and inhumane to continue using teaching methods that make students compete.

1. *Competition produces "winners"—but for every "winner," there are usually 29 "losers" in the average class.* Even if we recognize the "top 10," there are still 20 losers. Every time we compete, we are creating a situation in which at least two-thirds of our students will have a sense of failing. Against these kinds of odds, student motivation deteriorates.

148

2. *For most students, competitive activities are more selective than competitive.* Students know who the best spellers, readers, mathematicians, etc., are before they even begin competing. For the majority of the class it is only "a matter of time" before they have lost. To lose daily, monthly, and yearly results in a sense of worthlessness and incompetence for the average student.

3. *The main motivation in most competitive activities is to avoid failure.* Achieving success is often a secondary motivation. When students continually foresee their "doom" (failing), they become anxious. Not only does this interfere with their performance, but also it encourages choosing tasks with either a very high or a very low chance of success. If the chances for success are very high, they will be almost sure not to fail. If the chances for success are very low, no one can blame them for failing. Both of these choices reduce anxiety and can become unrealistic expectations that plague the student for life.

4. *Most interpersonal competitive activities are destructive to group cohesion and morale.* In order to "win," students must obstruct and defend against other students. They have hostile feelings toward those who do win because these students have relegated them to failing. Arguments over fairness and cheating are a constant blight to communication, positive regard, and trust.

5. *In competitive activities, the winners often feel guilty about beating their friends.* Also, students who are sensitive to their peers' rejection may fear the consequences of winning and, therefore, expend less effort and not achieve to their potential.

6. *For those who win most of the time, the emphasis on competition may have long-term, negative consequences on their personality development.* Because they are constantly given attention and approval for "winning," they may come to believe they are valued only for their "wins" and not for themselves. The result of such a belief is that they will have to continually "prove" themselves to be accepted. This can become a lifetime burden. The athlete who "can't hang it up" is not uncommon to this society.

7. *Continual competitive activities destroy intrinsic motivation for learning.* For competitive students, learning is a means to an end, the end being "winning." Learning for its own sake is irrelevant unless it helps the student "win," get high grades, or receive recognition. The internal question for such students is, "What *else* do I *have* to do?"—not, "What else do I *want* to do?" Knowledge that cannot be "used" to gain higher test scores, better grades, or more status becomes a waste of time. In this manner, lifelong learning is subverted to the "almighty A."

8. *Because lower-class students often lack basic skills in learning and/or do not value grades and other forms of "middle-class" recognition, competition in academics may be a disadvantage to their learning.* Such activities may increase their sense of alienation and rejection. Because lower-class students do not strive or yearn to compete, middle-class students may feel more distant from them with increasing discrimination and prejudice. "Blaming the victim" draws its daily lifeblood from competitive learning activities.

9. *The ability to compete is far less important to human survival than the ability to cooperate.* Our ecological system and energy crisis make this rather obvious. The vast majority of human interaction in all societies is not competitive, but cooperative. Communication, travel, exchange of goods and services, government, etc., would not be possible without extensive cooperation. At this time, one of the most significant characteristics that our students must attain for future life is the ability to functionally and effectively cooperate.

10. *Although popularly accepted, there is no research evidence that competition builds character and prepares the student for success in future competition.* In fact, there is research[18] that indicates competition does just the opposite. It appears that many athletes have a low interest in receiving support and concern from others, a low need to take care of others, and a low need for affiliation with others. The personality of the ideal athlete is not the result of constant competition, but rather it appears to come out of the ruthless selection process that occurs at all levels of sport.

At this point, I would like to issue a challenge. If you remain unconvinced of the detrimental consequences of competition, try writing out your reasons why competition is beneficial to most students. Then compare them to those found above. The verdict is yours.

I must add, however, that there are some activities for which competitive methods of learning can be useful and can facilitate student motivation. These types of instructional activities are skill practice and knowledge recall and review, with clearly defined rules for competing. Each student understands that the learning goal is *not* of great importance. Therefore, the student can accept either winning or losing. Other important expectancies for student participation are that they will have an equal chance of winning; they will enjoy the activity (win or lose); they will monitor the progress of competitors; and they will be able to compare ability, skill, or knowledge. In this situation, we are the major resource for assistance, support, and reinforcement.

A final word. Often, I hear teachers negate group competition but support self-competition. I oppose this. Students don't need to compete with themselves. They need to "be" themselves. Self-competition, in my opinion, is a manipulation that *forces* student effort under the guise of self-improvement. Self-competition implies, "Can't you make yourself better?" with the indirect intimidation of teacher observation and judgment.

Let students choose. Let students know themselves and what they want. We are not "seed planters"; we are "seed nurturers." It is all in the student to begin with. It will come out if we let it *be*.

Chapter 7

Reinforcement: The Finishing Touch

The last general motivation factor is reinforcement. Reinforcement is described and employed in this text in essentially the theoretical framework of B. F. Skinner. This means that it is used in an "operant" or "instrumental" sense where student behavior is emitted (mainly occurring spontaneously) and is instrumental in bringing about reinforcement. Therefore, reinforcement is defined[1] as an event or state of affairs that changes subsequent student behavior when it temporally follows an instance of that behavior. (For example, a student who is given praise for higher reading skill will tend to read more after that praise is given.)

Operationally, student motivation or behavior is acquired and its occurrence is regulated as a result of the contingent relationship between the response of the student and a consequent event. (For example, as the praise and amount of recognition for a given student task change, so student motivation or task performance will change to some extent.) This approach emphasizes observable behavior and mechanistic reasoning.

Although I have considerable respect for reinforcement theory and realize that it offers a comprehensive interpretation of student motivation with well-researched, insightful, and practical suggestions for teachers to follow,[2] I see it as limited in total scope and too sterile for the complexities and flexibility necessary to everyday teaching. Its dependency on observable behavior and its rigidity for mechanistic reasoning do not allow for the subtlety and intrinsic phenomenological world of human beings. However, I do see it as an important factor to consider in the ending of any learning event and will offer some strategies for its employment in facilitating student motivation. There are, however, a few more qualifications that I would like to add before initiating these suggestions.

Part of the problem with reinforcement theory is its holistic approach to motivation and learning. This is its greatest strength and its greatest weakness. On the one hand, it offers an entire methodology for teaching. Many of the ideas offered in previous chapters for facilitating motivation could be incorporated into its structure. But those chapters that deal with needs, affect, and competence would be severely limited. Thus, on the other hand, it is too rigid and confining. Students are infinitely complex; what they perceive tends to be subjective and phenomenological; their environments are rich and varied (even in school); what comes at the end is only part of the process of learning; the older the students become, the more they resent outside control; and many reinforcement approaches to motivation, such as programmed materials and behavior modification, have not been found by research to be the most effective methods of teaching all subject matter.

Finally, and maybe most importantly, are the differences as well as the interaction between *intrinsic* and *extrinsic* motivation. Extrinsic motivation emphasizes the value a student places on the ends (reinforcement) of an action and the probability of reaching those ends. In extrinsic motivation, the goal—not the "doing"—of the behavior is considered to be the reason for the performance of the behavior. So when we say that a student learned a skill or performed a task in order to get a reward, a higher grade, recognition, or praise from the teacher, we are accounting for that student's behavior primarily on the basis of extrinsic motivation. Intrinsic motivation refers to the pleasure or value associated with an activity itself. In intrinsic motivation, the "doing" of the behavior is considered to be the primary reason for the performance of that behavior. There is good evidence that many learning activities that involve manipulation, exploration, and information processing provide satisfaction in and of themselves. Students do read because it is enjoyable, and many also write, compute, and think for no other reason than the pleasure of those activities themselves. In these instances, we are inferring intrinsic motivation. Learning for the love of learning is essentially intrinsic motivation.

153

Although reinforcement theory makes valued extrinsic rewards contingent on learning behavior and has been found to be a generally effective motivational strategy, many educators question this practice. One reason is the issue of the transfer of learning behavior from a controlled environment to a noncontrolled environment. While reinforcement conditioning procedures have been quite effective in altering student behavior in a controlled setting, seldom have these changes been found to generalize to natural, nonreinforcing environments. If one of the major goals of education is preparation for life in the "real world," the effects of an exclusive reinforcement approach to teaching must be strongly questioned in light of these findings.

Another criticism appears to be the moral contention that "bribing" students to learn is inherently wrong. There is significant concern that through a total reinforcement approach to learning, students will be turned into "reinforcement junkies" who must always have something extra in order to learn. There is also the very real danger that extrinsic reward systems may interfere with and decrease intrinsic motivational properties within the learning behavior itself. There has been considerable research with regard to this issue.

In a representative study, Calder and Staw[3] describe the interaction between extrinsic and intrinsic motivational systems. In this study, male college students were asked to solve one of two sets of puzzles identical in all respects except the potential for intrinsic interest. One set of puzzles was pictorial and provocative while the other set was blank and neutral. To manipulate extrinsic rewards, half the subjects were promised one dollar for 20 minutes of labor, while for the other half of the subjects, money was not mentioned. The results of this study were these: When the task was initially interesting (i.e., picture puzzle activity), the introduction of money caused a reduction of task satisfaction; however, when the task was initially more neutral (i.e., blank puzzle activity), the introduction of money increased task satisfaction. Thus, it appears that in situations where the behavior is interesting and stimulating, to add an external reward becomes what might be called *overly sufficient justification* and decreases intrinsic motivation. However, in those instances where the behavior is not relatively interesting or stimulating, the addition of an external reward increases task satisfaction.

Staw's review of research on intrinsic and extrinsic motivation leads him to conclude that—

. . . there is no doubt that grades, gold stars and other such incentives can alter the direction and vigor of specific "in school" behaviors (e.g., getting students to complete assigned exercises by a particular date). But because of their effect on intrinsic motivation, extrinsic rewards may also weaken a student's general interest in learning tasks and decrease voluntary learning behavior that extends beyond the school setting. In essence, then, the extrinsic forces that work so well at motivating and controlling specific task behaviors may actually cause the extinction of these same behaviors within situations devoid of external reinforcers. This is an important consideration for educational organizations since most of an individual's learning activity will no doubt occur outside of the highly regulated and reinforcing setting of the classroom.[4]

It appears, based on current research, that in order to maintain students' intrinsic motivation, the use of extrinsic rewards must be carefully monitored. When a learning task is inherently interesting and would probably be performed without any external incentive, the addition of any extraneous rewards should be minimized. Only when the learning task appears too devoid of intrinsic value should the application of extrinsic systems of facilitating motivation be considered.

What this means to me is that when the other five general motivation factors of attitude, need, stimulation, affect, and competence have been incorporated within the learning activity, there will be little need for, and perhaps in some instances possible harm from, the addition of an extrinsic reinforcer. We must be careful that the magnitude of the extrinsic reinforcer and the emphasis we place on earning it are proportionately balanced with and congruent to the entire approach we use to facilitate student motivation.

Artificial Reinforcers

These are tangible or concrete materials, things, or symbols that are extrinsically provided by the teacher for learning behavior. Gold stars, prizes, candy, trinkets, certificates, trophies, points, and money are popular examples.

Strategy 1: *When any subject matter or learning activity is so aversive that the five other general motivation factors cannot facilitate student motivation, artificial reinforcers may be initially employed.* I will admit that it is possible to have students for whom the previously outlined strategies may not be entirely successful in facilitating their motivation to learn. They may be so negative or resistant to learning that merely initiating their attention is a major problem. I caution that this is rare but not impossible. Allowing a student to remain ignorant and continually in a state of nonlearning is more inhumane than employing artificial reinforcers. When a student is progressively "falling behind" and losing the grasp of a subject or skill, that student is in a state of continual punishment. The punishment of prolonged ignorance, the punishment of a lower self-concept, the punishment of poorer job potential, and the punishment of boredom and alienation are far worse than the use of artificial reinforcers.

However, such reinforcers should be used *to initiate* learning and to facilitate motivation in the early stages of the subject matter presentation. Eventually the subject or learning activity should begin to facilitate motivation through its own involvement with the student or else I would begin to question the validity of the subject and the learning process itself. For example, if after two months we cannot begin to withdraw the artificial reinforcers or employ the other general motivation factors, then the meaning and the value of the learning process or activity are highly questionable and "bribery" may, indeed, be taking place.

Three basic rules are helpful to the successful application of artificial reinforcers.

1. *Reinforce immediately*—Give reinforcement *while* the student is still learning what you want that student to learn. If you wait too long, you may be reinforcing stopping, inattentive behavior, or some nonlearning activity.

2. *Reinforce often with small amounts rather than frequently with large amounts*—Large amounts of anything that are given too often will lead to satiation. Smaller amounts of the reinforcer on a frequent basis will be less likely to satiate the student. The importance of frequency is that it will initially maintain the learning behavior at a high rate. The student can then become more thoroughly involved and the natural motivation properties of the subject matter will have a better chance to eventually intrinsically maintain the student's motivation.

3. *Reinforce small improvements in learning and motivation*— The most frequent error made by us is to demand too much before we

156

are willing to give the reinforcer. This leads to student discouragement and subverts the process. Start with a realistic first step. While we may feel that the student can and should do better, we must strengthen the best of what that student does *now*. We can help the student to raise standards as motivation increases. Reinforcement research has found that when working with problems or exercises, each student should get about nine out of ten responses correct to successfully maintain motivation.[5] This applies even at the college level.

Strategy 2: *Provide artificial reinforcers when they contribute to the natural flow of successful learning and provide closure with a positive ending.* Student motivation is enhanced when learning activities end on a "positive note." This means *not* that the learning behavior is carried out to achieve the positive ending (reinforcer), but that the valued closure is a symbolic and congruent part of the entire process. For example, finishing a learning unit with a class party or a special treat is an excellent way to affirm the efforts and contributions toward learning from all members of the class. As another example, a teacher may give stars or certificates of completion to enhance closure on a particular achievement such as the ending of a project or experimental production. The certificates or stars are not emphasized or held out as "carrots on a stick" during the major learning effort but are seen as ways to symbolize achievement and completion, much as diplomas or certificates of merit might be.

Sometimes we like to give something to our students to simply show our appreciation and affection for their effort and courage in learning. I would hate to see this ended because it appears "artificial." A surprise treat, a special movie, and a valued field trip are just some of the ways that we can "give" to our students and share our joy for them at the end of learning activities. Finally, there is the pure ecstasy of ending on a "high" when learning has been special and meaningful. This can range from the daily reading of an intriguing story at the end of a period of learning to the saving of the most entertaining activity until last so that students have a warm and joyful closure to their learning involvement.

In all of these examples, the emphasis is to use *positive* artificial reinforcers[6] as cohesive parts that fit naturally into the ending of learning activities. They are not to be used as the goals of learning or as extrinsic manipulators that take on greater importance than the learning itself.

Natural Consequences

This concept is reinforcement theory's interpretation of intrinsic motivation. According to Vargas[7] natural consequences are stimulus changes that are produced by (and are dependent on) the behavior of the individual who experiences them. Natural consequences are contrasted with "artificial" or "extrinsic" reinforcers that are provided by (and are dependent on) the behavior of others. Walking has the natural consequences of moving us toward certain goals and allowing us to see and experience new things. Reading a book has the natural consequence of producing new insights and expanded awareness. Thus, we say that we are interested in and enjoy reading. In this manner, reinforcement theory accounts for intrinsic motivation. However, the emphasis remains more on the product or result of learning than on the process (doing) of learning. Whether the performance of the learning behavior is a more powerful influence on student motivation than the intrinsic product of that performance is a debatable issue—e.g., Did I solve a problem for the joy of solving it, or did I solve it because I wanted an answer? My hunch is that both are part of the process and cannot be arbitrarily divided.

Strategy 1: *When learning has natural consequences, allow them to be congruently evident.* This means that we not *only* emphasize the result of a learning behavior, but also accept and highlight it as part of the learning process. Both the trip and the reaching of our destination are valued. Solving problems, gaining insights, making a discovery, and achieving greater awareness as a result of learning can be emphasized through discussion, evaluation, and planning for new learning. Much of this will be taken care of through the normal feedback procedures, but it does not hurt to sometimes add our acknowledgment and approval, especially in those instances where the natural consequences may not be readily apparent. This may be the case in small increments of progress on difficult tasks or not so readily understandable insights and discoveries—e.g., comparing student work from the past with recent improvement. Our clarification and focusing can help student motivation just as a speedometer helps us to know our progress and speed of travel.

Grades

Grades are defined in the context of this book in the traditional sense. This means that they are considered to be the normal five-scale symbols which historically have been A—excellent, B—good, C—average, D—poor, and F—failure. Whether or not they are extrinsic reinforcers depends on how they are given. If they are administered in an authoritarian manner and based solely on teacher standards with no input from the student, and if they are used to coerce student motivation, they are, indeed, extrinsic. However, if grades are based on mutual student–teacher learning goals with student participation in the evaluation process and are reflective of mutually agreed-upon criteria, they may be extrinsically given, but have a high intrinsic value because they reflect feedback and evaluation which are essential to any learning process.

Unfortunately, it appears that recent grading procedures, especially at the secondary level, are largely continued and maintained as extrinsic reinforcers. When grades are used in this manner, five criticisms are immediately apparent:

1. When grades are used to coerce student learning and are "held out" as the reason for studying, their extrinsic value may be the greatest singular influence on student motivation. This practice seriously diminishes the intrinsic motivational value of the subject matter for students, making learning an oppressive or manipulative effort to avoid low grades.

2. Because grades employed in this manner are used to control students, their sense of personal causation and their self-confidence are seriously impaired on a continual basis.

3. Grading in an extrinsic modality limits students' creativity and individuality of expression because students feel "forced" to give teachers exactly what they want.

4. When these grades are used to rank students or are given on the basis of a normal curve, student competition is enhanced and group cohesion suffers.

5. The continual reception of low grades by many students serves more as punishment than as reinforcement, and further discourages learning.

However, supporters of traditional grading procedures are quick to point out that student anxiety and lowered self-esteem are the result of low achievement, which grades only report and do not cause. They also argue that parents, students, and society want periodic, systematic summary evaluations, which, in essence, are the purpose of grades, so that students and those concerned with their learning can evaluate and compare their learning progress on a regular basis.

A number of alternatives to the traditional marking system have been established and appear promising. Nevertheless, these are used primarily at the elementary level and remain imperfect for all the purposes that regular grading procedures seem to satisfy. Some of the most popular are written evaluations, self-evaluation procedures, mastery and criterion-referenced approaches, and pass–fail grading.[8]

Personally, I don't like grading. I never have, and I doubt if I ever will. I continually hope that someone will find a better way to evaluate students and summarize those results in a regular manner that meets student and parent needs for feedback and comparison. At this moment, eliminating grades does not seem to be a realistic possibility on a nationwide basis. However, I want to strongly encourage and support those who continue to experiment with alternative approaches to assessing and reporting student achievement. Already these efforts at the elementary level have had a tremendous influence and may yet lead those of us in secondary education to a more humane and practical alternative. Some strategies to enhance the intrinsic value of traditional grading and to limit its negative extrinsic influence are found below.

Strategy 1: *Do not use traditional grades as the only form of feedback on student work.* First of all, grades give very little information, if any, that is really informative or helpful. Beyond saying that the student has passed or done well, a grade as a form of feedback can give either no more information—or only negative information, if it is low. Secondly, to continually place grades on student papers, projects, and general efforts consistently reminds the student of that eventual report card marking and increases the pressure and extrinsic value of the grade. (The subfactor of "Awareness of Progress and Mastery" has many strategies to provide feedback in a more constructive manner.)

Strategy 2: *Discuss with and involve your students in the grading procedure you intend to employ.* If students have had some participation in the decision making concerning what their grading criteria and the general expectations for grading are going to be, they can feel personal causation. To a certain extent, we, as teachers, will be limited as to what degree students can determine this, but, nonetheless, if we are straightforward and allow for certain variations that relate to their values and understanding, we have taken a step toward the enhancement of student responsibility for learning. Also, their fullest comprehension of the rationale and criteria for grading will be of benefit to them in determining what they want to do, as well as why they may attain the grades they do.

Strategy 3: *Use student self-evaluation as part of your grading decision.* Again, this enhances a sense of personal causation on the part of the learner. Very few students will speak against themselves, and this should not be expected by us. (The Fifth Amendment protects this right.) But we can get a sense of their self-assessment, and use it as a significant part in determining their grade. Also, it allows for an honest exchange that few paper-and-pencil techniques can ever provide.

Strategy 4: *Do not grade on a normal curve.* Classes aren't normal. Grading on a curve encourages competition. It prevents individualization and mastery learning. It is a highly irrational process in terms of current learning theory and research.

Strategy 5: *Have your grading process supportive of your teaching style.*[9] If you individualize and use cooperative goal structures, use a *categorical system* of assigning report card grades. This means that you and your students agree on a set of standards, and you judge the achievement of each student against those standards. *Comparative systems* are those that compare the performance of one student against another before arriving at a judgment for a grade. While these may be appropriate for competitive learning situations, they can undermine individualized and cooperative efforts to teach.

In some instances, you may have to use a multidimensional approach to report card grading that employs both categorical and comparative systems of evaluation. This is often because parents and society demand comparison. Under such circumstances there are two alternatives. One is to give two grades. The first grade is for individual and cooperative student achievement, and the second grade is for comparative student achievement. This way a student can see how she/he does by her or his own standards, as well as how she/he does compared to a normative standard that includes all the students in

161

the class. The second approach is to assign a percentage of the final grade for individual and cooperative learning and a percentage of the final grade for comparative learning. For example, 50% of the student's grade accounts for learning in individual and cooperative situations, which is at the A level, and 50% accounts for the student's learning on a comparative basis, which is at a C level. Thus, the student would receive a B on her or his report card. If either of these approaches is used, the student must be well informed on the grading approach and be able to understand the process being applied.

Regardless of the particular form of grading that you employ, it still appears to be an imperfect system. Therefore, continual communication with students on this matter is necessary. They need the freedom to question grades and various forms of assessment to relieve their anxiety and doubt. The report card is often the last and probably the most significant conclusion to any learning endeavor in American education. Its success as a positive influence on student motivation will depend primarily on the care that is taken to define the system of grading and on the consistency and fairness with which that system is used.

Chapter 8

The Beginning at the End: Making It Work

Now that each general motivation factor and its related motivation subfactors and strategies have been described and discussed, you have probably begun to wonder, "How can all this be effectively organized to help me facilitate student motivation?" One of the problems mentioned earlier regarding motivation has been its complexity and multiplicity of approaches and strategies—all of which have to be adapted to your situation, your students, your goals, and your own teaching philosophy and personality. Where to begin can seem to be a monumental question in and of itself. This book has outlined 23 motivation subfactors as well as 82 related strategies (see Figure 4).

My suggestion for dealing with all of these possibilities is to encourage motivational planning. Just as we make lesson plans, I strongly believe that we must also make related motivation plans. Meaning does not exist without structure—and this applies to *both* learning and motivation. To be well organized in *what* we present to our students gives significance to the content of their learning experience; *how* effectively we present this content enables the process of motivated student learning. If I have any criticism of modern teaching methods, it is that we have placed emphasis on the objectives and content of learning without placing relatively equal stress on the process and motivational aspects of learning. Figuratively, we have, indeed, drawn the horse to water, but we have not paid enough attention to how to help it drink.

Before I begin a more descriptive discussion of motivational planning, I want to encourage what I believe to be one of the major uses of this book—continued evolution of ourselves as professional teachers. I do not believe that teachers are made or born. We come to the profession usually as young students who are entering our third year of college experience. At this time, we begin our introduction and training within the teaching profession with college education classes and possibly some initial field experience. After two to three more years of classes, training, and intern teaching, we are given a degree and some form of certification. Then most of us are on our own, and if we are lucky enough to get a job, we enter the classroom, close the door, and try to "make it" in what is always an awesome and often lonely challenge.

Some of us are initially successful, relating well to children, handling discipline efficiently, and effectively communicating our subject matter. We may seem to be "born" teachers. Others among us start with a struggle. We may have serious motivation and discipline problems, and wonder about our capabilities. For those of us in this group, it may take two to three years before we feel secure and adept at our profession. We are the "made" teachers. And some of us never make it. We may stay or leave, depending on economic necessity, other opportunities, and a host of varied influential factors. But from my experience, the real test comes sometime after the third year of teaching, when not only have we changed through experience and maturation but also so have our society, our schools, and our children through the natural evolution of cultural and social transformation.

Our job description may not be new, but almost everything else is. Do we still have our enthusiasm and commitment? Can we relate to today's children—and parents and institutions? Are we allowing ourselves to change and broaden our perspectives and skills? Or do we feel out of place, alienated from our work, and unmotivated for the challenge that may feel more like a daily struggle? Just as the world evolves, so does education, and, therefore, so must teachers continue their development. What worked and seemed secure before may not be so now. It is an evolutionary process: Effective teachers evolve and continue; if they do not, their chances of stagnating and becoming disillusioned and ineffective are considerably greater. Therefore, this book is written to be used to affirm what we do well, and to refine and improve those skills and abilities that our awareness encourages us to act upon.

Self-Awareness and Motivation

One way to begin this process is to consider five areas that significantly affect our approach to student motivation. Take a few minutes for each section and give yourself time to answer the questions and feel your emotions as you integrate and evaluate your various thoughts and feelings. (Writing out responses to each section can clarify and make the entire process more concrete and applicable.)

1. *Your perception of your students as learners:* (a) Do you see them as naturally curious, intelligent, and creative? List six teaching behaviors that indicate this. (b) Do you trust them to learn? How? (c) Do you allow them to be responsible for their own learning? How?

2. *Your perception of your teaching situation:* (a) Do you feel free to be creative and imaginative in your teaching situation? If not, why? (b) What are the three major advantages and the three major obstacles in your teaching situation? (c) How is your teaching situation changing? How are you changing with it?

3. *Your goals as a teacher:* (a) What do you specifically want to happen as a result of your teaching? List and rank your five most important goals as a teacher. (b) How are you accomplishing these?

4. *Your assumptions about student motivation:* (a) What does motivation mean to you? (b) Describe the behavior of a motivated student. What does she/he specifically do to let you know she/he is motivated? List five observable behaviors of a motivated student. How often do you see these in your classroom?

5. *Your perception of yourself as a motivating teacher:* (a) List the top six things that you often do to facilitate student motivation. (b) Consider the best and the worst lessons that you teach. In your opinion, what makes the former motivating and what makes the latter unmotivating for students? (c) Complete this sentence as often as you can as you believe your students would: "My teacher helps me to feel motivated because she/he . . . ."

After you have reflected upon and completed the five areas, return to each of the five sections and complete this sentence for each:

"Answering and reflecting upon these statements and questions makes me realize that I . . . ."

You will now have five declarative statements that personally relate to student motivation and your role as a teacher. I do not know what they will say to you, and there are no predictable answers. My hope is that they will help to stimulate and to clarify what you are and what you want from what this book has to offer.

Inventory of Motivation Strategies

Now I want to extend an invitation to you: Conduct your own personal inventory of motivation strategies. This is time consuming and laborious, but it is also most worthwhile. In my experience, most teachers have not had the opportunity to carefully and critically examine their teaching behavior in relation to motivation. This is not because we have not wanted to (quite the contrary, because most of us are eager for increased self-awareness regarding motivation and learning), but rather because such an instrument or listing did not previously exist. Well, now it does, and here are some possible advantages in completing the inventory:

1. You will have an increased awareness of what you functionally do to facilitate student motivation.

2. You will have an increased awareness of what you do not do to facilitate student motivation.

3. You will have a more accurate sense of possible new strategies that you may want to incorporate or strengthen in your teaching.

4. You will have a more accurate sense of possible strategies that you may want to eliminate or lessen in your teaching.

5. You will have a more accurate sense of which general motivation factors and their related subfactors are part of your approach to student motivation.

6. You will be able to more effectively plan your strategies to facilitate student motivation.

It appears that anywhere from one to two hours are necessary to sensitively complete and evaluate the inventory.

Well, let's begin.

166

1. The first step is to return to Figure 4—The Diagnostic Motivation Chart. (You may want to duplicate a copy of it for writing purposes.)

2. In Column 3 is a series of motivation strategies that are listed for each motivation subfactor.

3. After reading each strategy, evaluate how often you employ the strategy in your daily teaching, and code the strategy according to one of five possible categories: A—Always, O—Often, S—Sometimes, Se—Seldom, or N—Never.

4. Do this for each strategy in the entire chart. After you have completed this process, you will have some sense of how often or to what degree you employ these strategies in your regular teaching.

5. Then return to each strategy and initiate a second code of evaluation. This judgment is based on what you want to do about your facilitation of student motivation, given your awareness of your current employment of the strategy. One of the following four categories is possible:

C—Continue: You have decided that the current employment of the strategy is satisfactory.

E—Enhance: You want to improve or increase the use of this strategy.

B—Begin: You are not using this strategy and want to initiate some employment of it.

L—Lessen: You feel this strategy is used too often or you prefer some other strategy in its place and want to lessen its employment.

See Figure 15 for an example of this process with the strategies outlined for "Expectancy for Success."

6. After completing the second coding, not only do you know how often you employ the various strategies, but also you have some idea about what you want to do regarding their future use.

You may find from doing this evaluation that you use the strategies of certain general motivation factors or their subfactors heavily while you use others seldom or never. This may give some insight into both your strengths and your weaknesses in facilitating

167

Figure 15

1.	Interview the student.	S (Sometimes)	C (Continue)
2.	Use goal-setting methods.	Se (Seldom)	E (Enhance)
3.	Use contracting methods.	O (Often)	C (Continue)
4.	Use programmed materials.	O (Often)	L (Lessen)

student motivation. Since I believe that each general motivation factor can be used to some extent in facilitating student motivation in any learning situation, I encourage you to pay special attention to those general factors that appear to have strategies that are seldom or never used. This may be indicative of some deficit in your overall approach to student motivation.

My strongest caution is against being overwhelmed by this process. You may find many motivation strategies that you want to enhance, begin, or lessen. My suggestion is to rank these strategies according to those that seem to have the most personal value as well as the greatest probability of being successful. Then begin by making no more than a few concrete changes, based on your highest-ranked strategies, until you feel that your teaching style and students have positively adapted to these adjustments. Then you can incorporate more motivation changes that appear desirable. Again, I remind you that teaching is an evolutionary process and that the use of motivation strategies tends to follow this principle.

Basic Motivation Planning

After having read the previous chapters, as well as having completed an inventory of your motivation strategies, you will have a better sense of which motivation subfactors and related strategies you may wish to employ in your planning to facilitate student motivation. As I have mentioned, each learning situation is unique and has its own particular time frame. It is quite possible to spend a few lessons or even a few days by devoting our motivation planning to the beginning of a learning situation. In such a case, we would spend our effort in utilizing the strategies of the general motivation factors of attitudes and needs. The same is also true for the middle and ending of learning situations where stimulation and affect or competence and reinforcement would be more thoroughly employed.

In the examples that follow, I have considered each learning situation as a complete unit with beginning, during, and ending time phases so that all aspects of the motivation model may be illustrated for planning. I realize that any complete learning situation can occur in minutes, hours, days, or months. The time and qualitative differences between a short lecture and a long-term project are immense. No matter how these types of learning might remain different in terms of time and quality, they do deserve some motivation planning to facilitate continued student involvement and effort. My goal is not to confine the teacher to some form of perfect time regimentation, but to encourage the idea that certain motivation strategies have more value and impact if planned with a sense of timing.

EXAMPLE 1: A high school history teacher is presenting a 60-minute lecture/discussion on the Age of Pericles. Her or his objective is essentially information processing. She/he wants the students to hear and to learn about this period of ancient Greek history in terms of what the dominant philosophy of this culture was, who the major artists, scientists, and leaders were, and how this period influenced future civilization.

The motivation plan might be:

MOTIVATION PLAN FOR EXAMPLE 1

	MOTIVA-TION FACTORS	*MOTIVATION STRATEGIES*[1]	*FUNCTIONAL STRATEGIES*
B E G I N N I N G	(*Attitudes*) Attitude toward the subject and learning situation	1. Make the conditions that surround the subject positive.	1. Pass among the students a set of replicas of artifacts from this period of history—i.e., statues, coins, pottery, pictures of dress, sporting events, weapons, etc.
		2. Model enthusiasm for the subject taught.	2. Relate feelings and experiences regarding a vacation in Greece.

169

MOTIVA-TION FACTORS	MOTIVATION STRATEGIES[1]	FUNCTIONAL STRATEGIES
B **E** **G** **I** **N** **N** **I** **N** **G**	**5.** Make the first experience with the subject matter as positive as possible.	**5.** Read a humorous episode from Aristophanes' *The Birds* to illustrate the sense of humor particular to this period of history.
(Needs) Safety needs	**3.** Create a learning environment that is organized and orderly.	**3.** Prepare and outline the lecture.
(Stimulation) Interest and involvement	**2.** Find out student interests and relate learning to them.	**2.** Ask the class which of the Greek artifacts they found particularly interesting, and, based on this information, explain more about the replicas.
D **U** **R** **I** **N** **G**	**3.** Use humor, examples, analogies, stories, and questions to facilitate the active participation of students in your lectures and demonstrations.	**3.** Compare Athenian democracy to American democracy; compare ancient Greek artists and writers to present-day artists and writers; and compare Athenian leaders to modern-day leaders.
(Affect) Confluency	**2.** Have the students imagine and deal with learning experiences as they relate to their real lives.	**2.** Ask students to imagine and discuss what about Athenian life they would desire to find and choose for their present life-styles.
(Competence) **E** **N** **D** **I** **N** **G** Awareness of progress and mastery	**4.** Help the learners to realize how to operationalize in daily living what has been learned.	**4.** Relate to the class what the Athenian ideals of freedom and responsibility mean with regard

MOTIVA-TION FACTORS	MOTIVATION STRATEGIES[1]	FUNCTIONAL STRATEGIES
		to justice and to student and teacher rights in school settings.
E N D I N G	(Reinforcement)	
	Natural consequences	1. When learning has natural consequences, allow them to be congruently evident.	1. Have students form small groups and conclude by discussing the most significant insight that they gained from the lecture.

The above example contains at least one subfactor for each of the six general motivation factors. Each of the motivation strategies is correlated by number to those factors and strategies found in the Diagnostic Motivation Chart (see Figure 4). In this example, 9 strategies are used out of a possible 82. It is quite likely that more or fewer strategies could be used, depending on teacher goals, student experience, the learning situation, time involved, etc. The functional strategies are what the teacher would do to actualize the motivation strategies. With experience and practice, it is probable that it will be necessary to plan and write only the general motivation factors and the functional strategies in advance of the learning situation. Again, I want to encourage use of all six general motivation factors in any motivation planning scheme. The next two examples are self-explanatory and further illustrate motivation planning for different situations and age groups.

EXAMPLE 2: The teacher is an elementary school teacher in a self-contained homeroom. She/he is facilitating a unit on fractions. The objective is to have the students at the end of the unit add and subtract mixed fractions (e.g., $\frac{1}{2} + \frac{1}{4} =$ _____, $\frac{1}{3} - \frac{1}{6} =$ _____, $1\frac{1}{2} + 2\frac{1}{3} =$ _____, $3\frac{1}{2} - 2\frac{1}{4} =$ _____) at a 90 percent achievement level. This is conceivably a two- to four-week endeavor.

The motivation plan might be:

MOTIVATION PLAN FOR EXAMPLE 2

	MOTIVATION FACTORS	*MOTIVATION STRATEGIES*	*FUNCTIONAL STRATEGIES*
	(Attitudes)		
	Attitude toward the subject and learning situation	**1.** Make the conditions that surround the subject positive.	**1.** Give students puzzles of shapes (circles, triangles, etc.), people, and things (trees, houses, etc.) to work on to positively demonstrate how fractions can make up wholes.
		2. Model enthusiasm for the subject.	**2.** Relate a story of how as a member of a family you are constantly using fractions of things (money, food, etc.) to share with your family. Then bring a treat (cake, pie, etc.) and have the class help you to divide it to share among them.
BEGINNING		**4.** Positively confront the possible erroneous beliefs, expectations, and assumptions that may underly the negative student attitude.	**4.** Ask students how many have heard that fractions are really difficult to do and discuss with them their feelings and expectancies.
	Attitude toward the self	**1.** Guarantee successful learning.	**1.** Segment the initial paper-and-pencil task into achievable increments and give immediate feedback.
		2. Encourage the student.	**2.** Circulate among the students, acknowledging their effort and progress and helping those who need it.
	Expectancy for success	**4.** Use programmed materials.	**4.** Give students the programmed unit on fractions to practice skills

MOTIVATION FACTORS	MOTIVATION STRATEGIES	FUNCTIONAL STRATEGIES
		and individualize progress.
(Needs) Safety needs	**2.** Reduce or remove components of the learning environment that lead to failure or fear.	**2.** Organize a tutorial assistance plan by which students who are having difficulty can receive immediate help from you, a teacher's aide, or a fellow student.
Esteem needs	**4.** Plan activities to allow students to publicly display and share their talents and work.	**4.** Organize a sharing-fraction project by which teams of students creatively share something (help, time, skits, music, etc.) and demonstrate their knowledge of fractions.
(Stimulation) Variety	**4.** Change the style as well as the content of the learning activities.	**4.** Throughout the unit, mix the style of learning to include paper-and-pencil tasks, board work, concrete materials (puzzles, blocks, etc.), and oral problem solving.
Interest and involvement	**4.** Whenever possible, make student reaction and involvement essential parts of the learning process—i.e., problem solving, games, role playing, simulation, etc.	**4.** Use games and creative problems to challenge and invite daily student participation.
(Affect) Confluency	**3.** Use student concerns to organize content and to develop themes and teaching procedures.	**3.** Discuss with students what is the most difficult thing or activity that they have to "share" in their daily lives. Demonstrate and then invite students to use their

B E G I N N I N G (alongside Needs section)

D U R I N G (alongside Stimulation/Affect section)

173

MOTIVA- TION FACTORS	MOTIVATION STRATEGIES	FUNCTIONAL STRATEGIES
D U R I N G Climate	**2.** Use a cooperative goal structure to maximize student involvement and sharing.	knowledge of fractions to solve and understand this kind of problem. **2.** Have teams of students solve fraction problems with one member of the team responsible for diagnosing the problem (addition or subtraction), another responsible for finding the common denominators, another for working it through, and another for checking the answer. Alternate roles.
(Competence) Awareness of progress and mastery	**1.** Provide consistent feedback regarding mastery of learning.	**1.** Use tutors, answer sheets, and diagnostic and formative tests to give immediate feedback and assistance to students.
E N D I N G Responsibility	**1.** Acknowledge and affirm the student's responsibility in completing the learning task.	**1.** Congratulate students for finishing particular assignments, projects, and subunits. Acknowledge their perseverance and cooperativeness. Discuss with them what part of doing fractions seemed the most difficult and how they conquered the problem.
(Reinforce- ment) Artificial reinforcers	**2.** Provide artificial reinforcers when they contribute to the natural flow of successful learning and provide closure with a positive ending.	**2.** End the unit with a "Fraction Festival." Fraction off treats and use fraction games and sharing activities to celebrate the end of the unit.

EXAMPLE 3: A junior high school teacher is teaching a unit on American government to a social studies class. She/he is individualizing projects for students. One of the students is particularly interested in working on an enterprise that deals with the judicial system. This will be a six-week endeavor.

The motivation plan might be:

MOTIVATION PLAN FOR EXAMPLE 3

MOTIVATION FACTORS	*MOTIVATION STRATEGIES*	*FUNCTIONAL STRATEGIES*
(Attitudes)		
Attitude toward the self	3. Emphasize the student's personal causation in learning.	3. Plan and set goals for learning according to student choice with an agreed-upon evaluation procedure. Analyze with the student her or his strengths and abilities as well as any potential blocks to the project's completion. Ask the student for a commitment.
Expectancy for success	2. Use goal-setting methods.	2. Follow the goal-setting plan found on page 54.
	3. Use contracting methods.	3. Finalize with a contract that includes observable results of learning, proficiency expected, and resources to be used —e.g., a five-page report with three major insights and an evaluation of the system based on standards of justice and equality.

B
E
G
I
N
N
I
N
G

MOTIVA-TION FACTORS	MOTIVATION STRATEGIES	FUNCTIONAL STRATEGIES
B E G I N N I N G (Needs) Self-actuali-zation needs	**3.** Provide the opportunity for self-discovery through freedom of choice in the learning situation with emphasis on risk taking, problem solving, experimentation, and self-evaluation.	**3.** Arrange for a large component of the project to be open ended and facilitative of exploration and discovery. Serve as a consultant to the student with periodic meetings to provide guidance and feedback—e.g., compare the U.S. judicial system to the Russian system; meet half an hour once a week.
D U R I N G (Stimulation) Questions	**1.** Limit the use of knowledge questions, and selectively increase the use of comprehension, application, analysis, synthesis, and evaluation questions.	**1.** During meetings, ask the student: (a) How could the U.S. judicial system be improved? (b) What part of the system seems most important to the country's welfare? (c) How does the Supreme Court function? (d) Why should judges be elected? (e) Is the jury system fair?
Disequilibrium	**3.** Play the devil's advocate.	**3.** During meetings, confront the student with: (a) the high cost of lawyers that favors the upper and middle classes; (b) the lack of minority judges; (c) the extensive delays of trials; (d) the police frustration with plea bargaining; and (e) the bribery of judges.

MOTIVA-TION FACTORS	MOTIVATION STRATEGIES	FUNCTIONAL STRATEGIES
(Affect) Confluency	**1.** Have the student "live out" the cognitive concepts presented by experiencing them in the classroom setting. **3.** Use student concerns to organize content and to develop themes and teaching procedures.	**1.** and **3.** Organize and conduct a mock trial based on a recent news event that is of vital interest to the class. Have students role-play lawyers, jury, defendants, etc., with the project student acting as judge and facilitator.
(Competence) Awareness of progress and mastery	**2.** Use constructive criticism.	**2.** Periodically check the student's rough draft and outline of the report to give feedback and positive ways to improve it.
Responsibility	**2.** Use a competence checklist for student self-rating.	**2.** Use the competence checklist found on page 146. After the student has completed it, discuss the results with the student.
	3. Acknowledge the risk taking and challenge involved in the learning accomplishment.	**3.** Receive the student's report and have a meeting to discuss it, as well as her or his overall work. Acknowledge and affirm the student's efforts toward exploration and discovery in producing it—e.g., your personal reactions to the mock trial and insights found in the report.

D U R I N G (marginal label for first row)

E N D I N G (marginal label)

177

MOTIVA-TION FACTORS	MOTIVATION STRATEGIES	FUNCTIONAL STRATEGIES
(Reinforcement)		
ENDING Grades	2. Discuss with and involve your students in the grading procedure you intend to employ. 3. Use student self-evaluation as part of your grading decision.	2. and 3. While discussing the student's report and general effort, make special notice of how the particular agreements in the contract were met and how these relate to the grade to be received. Ask the student's opinion in regard to evaluation of the work completed—e.g., How do you feel about what you did? Do you think you met the criteria we agreed on? Arrive at the grade as a result of your mutual discussion of the total project.

The above examples stress three guidelines that I want to encourage for the successful facilitation of student motivation:

1. Planning of motivation strategies along a time frame that maximizes their effectiveness.

2. Use of motivation strategies that relate to each of the six general motivation factors.

3. Use of particular strategies that relate to teacher personality, learning situation, subject matter, and student characteristics.

I have given the rationale for each of these guidelines earlier and hope these examples clarify their meaning. These examples are given to highlight these guidelines, but in no way are they written as complete and final descriptions. It is quite possible that you could find better and more inventive means to approach student motivation for these particular instances. These examples illustrate what might be possible and what is structurally necessary. They are not written as precise models to follow, but rather as samples that clarify and suggest.

Prevention and Restorative Motivation Planning

Another use of this text and its contained materials is to avert the development of motivation problems before they become serious disabilities for teacher and student alike. Related to this aspect is the restoration of student motivation where significant problems do exist. I prefer the concept of restoration to remediation when motivation is discussed. My belief is that motivation for learning is a human self-preserving capacity that exists from birth and is found in young children in their natural curiosity and need for competence and stimulation. It is there to begin with and, when lacking, has been eroded, fragmented, or stagnated through oppressive and impoverished learning situations, failure, defeat, and/or lack of stimulation. Therefore, student motivation is not something to remedy but to restore to the vitality that comes with entry into the human species.

Whenever we have a motivational problem or concern about our students, we must first clarify what is it that we want. Do we want the student to try something? Do we want the student to complete something? Do we want the student to be enthusiastic about something? Do we want the student to persevere at something? It can be a single goal or a combination of goals for us. But unless we are clear about what it is that we want, our chances of resolving the issue are significantly lessened. For example, do we want something *for* the student or *from* the student? Concerns that deal with things *from* the student are usually centered on performance, products, or material learned. Concerns that deal with things *for* the student are usually focused on student attitude, emotion, and volition. If our students are enthusiastic, will we be satisfied if they do not complete their work, or if our students complete their work, will we be satisfied if they do so without enthusiasm? Although student performance and attitude need not be separate, I present these questions to illustrate the necessity for clear comprehension of our goals to help us to gain satisfaction from our work with students. We often place our students as well as ourselves in self-defeating positions when we are unclear about our expectancies and desires.

After we have a distinct awareness of what it is that we want to happen in the area of student motivation, we can then shift our focus to the student's perception of the learning situation. In this manner, we can employ the diagnostic questions found in Figure 4. Each of these is written *with the student's point of view in mind.* We are not to ask these questions of ourselves but to imagine as empathically as possible how the student would answer them. This is a vitally important approach. Many times we can fool ourselves and subvert our best intentions by lacking the student's perspective regarding motivation. But if we honestly try to place ourselves in the student's vantage point, we can understand more clearly the dynamics that are affecting her or him. Therefore, each diagnostic question is to be used in an empathic sense to attempt to sensitively probe those general factors or subfactors of motivation that may not be functioning effectively to positively influence student motivation.

The diagnostic questions, either singularly or in combination, are not a refined form of instrumentation that gives precise specification of what strategies to employ. What they can do, if used sensitively, is to provide a general designation of possible motivation factors that are not successfully operating and to indicate the related motivation strategies that have a probability of preventing further motivation problems from occurring and of restoring student motivation to a higher level.

There are 23 diagnostic questions in Figure 4. Each is related to a specific motivation subfactor as well as to a set of motivation strategies. If you are experiencing problems with student motivation, these questions can be used to help you to more accurately perceive motivational influences upon the student. If the motivational influences of the related motivation subfactor appear to be lacking, absent, negative, or nonfunctioning, the related motivation strategies can be employed to facilitate student motivation.

For example, you may believe that a particular student has a negative attitude in math, but you need to find out the specific focus of that attitude. By asking the following four diagnostic questions under the general motivation factor of "Attitudes" (see Figure 4), you can better understand which motivation subfactor is problematic and then decide upon which of the related strategies you want to employ.

180

1. What are the student's perception and feeling toward the teacher? [She/he likes me and we relate well.]

2. What are the student's perception and feeling toward the subject and learning situation? [She/he usually enjoys math and has been enthusiastic in the past.]

3. What are the student's sense of worth and capabilities in the learning situation? [She/he does seem somewhat uncertain with this new material.]

4. How well does the student honestly and objectively expect to do in the learning situation? [She/he might expect to fail.]

In this example, it would appear that motivation strategies related to the subfactors of "Attitude Toward the Self" and "Expectancy for Success" are likely to facilitate the student's motivation. It is quite possible that encouragement and the use of programmed materials would help to restore the student's motivation and reduce the negative attitude.

Another hypothetical case might be where history students have a positive attitude and want to learn, but complain of being, or appear to be, bored. This may be a stimulation problem, and the use of diagnostic questions for subfactors under this general motivation factor may prove helpful to find strategies to resolve the problem (see Figure 4).

1. How are the various subtopics and subunits of learning effectively introduced and connected? [They seem to be able to follow my lectures and respond when I do present alerting cues.]

2. What is there that is continually different about the learner's environment and activities? [Not too much, I usually lecture most of the time.]

3. How often does the learner figuratively step into and become a part of the learning activity? [Not very often.]

4. In the learner's perception, how stimulating and provocative are the questions being discussed? [When I do ask questions, the students seem to be more responsive.]

181

5. How is the learner confronted with information or processes that are different, novel, contrasting, or discrepant from what she/he already knows or has experienced? [When I play the devil's advocate, we have our most alive and interesting discussions.]

In this illustration, it seems that motivation strategies related to the subfactors of "Variety" and "Interest and Involvement" would have the greatest probability of facilitating student motivation. Shifting interaction between yourself and students and between the students themselves during classroom presentations; changing the style as well as the content of the learning activity; and making student reaction and involvement an essential part of the learning process—i.e., problem solving, games, role playing, simulation, etc.—are strategies likely to restore student motivation and prevent boredom.

One of the problems with the use of the diagnostic questions is that when there is a motivation problem, there is often what I call a *motivation depression*. That is, student motivation is so low that it appears that very few or even none of the general motivation factors is positively operating, and, therefore, most of the answers to the diagnostic questions are negative. So many things appear to be wrong that we may not know where to start or which strategies to select.

Other than playing our hunches and using our intuition, there are at least three rational things that can be done.

First, we can take advantage of the two other diagnostic surveys found in this text. These are the climate survey and the self-diagnostic questionnaire (Figures 12 and 13) found in Chapter 5 under the subfactor of "Climate." The use of these devices may help to pinpoint some approaches that may have a higher probability of successfully facilitating student motivation.

Secondly, we can ask ourselves, *when* does student motivation for learning seem to decline or erode? If it is right from the start or at the beginning of what we teach, then it would seem most helpful to initiate diagnostic questions and related strategies for the general motivation factors of "Attitudes" and "Needs." If we can start what we are teaching with positive student motivation, but then seem to bog down during the main body of the learning material, diagnostic questions and related strategies for the general motivation factors of "Stimulation" and "Affect" may lead to some resolution of the problem. And if we appear to have student motivation problems occurring mainly at the ending or with completion of the learning activity, the diagnostic questions and related strategies for the general motivation factors of "Competence" and "Reinforcement" may prove most helpful.

Thirdly, and most importantly, we can honestly and openly discuss with our students what they think and feel the problem might be. We can use the diagnostic questions to stimulate their thinking and offer related strategies for their judgment and selection. Motivation, as well as learning, is a teacher–student goal for which we each share a part of the responsibility. Use of the strategies related to the motivation subfactors of "Feelings" and "Climate" in Chapter 5 should aid this approach.

Whatever means we use to employ the diagnostic questions, once we have some degree of assurance that we have located the motivation subfactors that are in need of improvement, we then select the related motivation strategies that appear to have optimal influence in preventing the motivation problem and in restoring higher levels of student motivation. These we emphasize within our daily motivation plans for the student. The following two examples illustrate this.

EXAMPLE 1: A middle elementary teacher in a self-contained classroom has a student with whom the teacher believes she/he has a personality conflict. The student does not appear to like the teacher and refuses to do assignments or does them poorly without care or precision. The teacher wants the student to trust her or him, to sincerely attempt the work, and to produce realistic effort toward completion of the assignments. A diagnostic interview with the student reveals that the student does not trust the teacher and feels insecure in working with her or him. The teacher selects motivation strategies related to the subfactors of "Attitude Toward the Teacher," "Expectancy for Success," "Safety Needs," "Feelings," "Climate," and "Responsibility" to emphasize and incorporate in daily motivation plans for this student.

The motivation plan might be:

RESTORATIVE MOTIVATION PLAN FOR EXAMPLE 1

MOTIVA-TION FACTORS	MOTIVATION STRATEGIES	FUNCTIONAL STRATEGIES
B E G I N N I N G		
(*Attitudes*) Attitude toward the teacher	**1.** Establish a relationship with the student by sharing something of value with the student.	**1.** Give the student daily positive attention on an individual basis for at least five minutes in the morning and five minutes in the afternoon.
	2. Listen to the student with empathic regard.	**2.** During the time that the student is receiving individual attention, engage her or him in conversation and demonstrate acceptance and understanding of the meaning and feeling of her or his statements.
	3. Treat the student with warmth and acceptance.	**3.** Whenever possible be available to the student and ask her or his help to do something at least once every three days.
Expectancy for success	**3.** Use contracting methods.	**3.** Use a contract system for daily assignments.
(*Needs*) Safety needs	**2.** Reduce or remove components of the learning environment that lead to failure or fear.	**2.** Use a mastery approach with the student for learning basic skills.
D U R I N G		
(*Stimulation*) (*Affect*) Feelings	Daily Motivation Plan **3.** When a student seems unmotivated, simply describe her/his behavior and ask an open-ended question to facilitate understanding and resolution of the issue.	Daily Motivation Plan **3.** If assignments are late or poorly done, describe the situation and ask the student for clarification.

184

MOTIVA-TION FACTORS	MOTIVATION STRATEGIES	FUNCTIONAL STRATEGIES
D U R I N G Climate	1. Use Gibb's supportive communication behaviors to facilitate a positive climate.	1. Avoid judgmental or evaluative behavior with the student. Be descriptive and accepting.
E N D I N G *(Competence)* Responsibility	1. Acknowledge and affirm the student's responsibility in completing the learning task.	1. Congratulate the student upon completion of the assignments. Acknowledge the perseverance involved. Celebrate the first completed assignment.
(Reinforcement)	Daily Motivation Plan	Daily Motivation Plan

EXAMPLE 2: A high school English literature teacher notices that although the semester has gotten off to a good start, things seem to be bogging down in class. Discussions seem to include fewer participants, and there is an air of tension in the room during these sessions. Students appear to enjoy what they're reading and are interested in the novels' themes and insights. Often the class starts well, but when discussion occurs, there is a "let down" and the mood of the students shifts downward.

The teacher wants to prevent further decline of student motivation in the class, especially during discussions. She/he wants more overall enthusiasm and an increased number of participants during discussion sessions. After conducting a climate survey, the teacher finds that students rate the classroom atmosphere high in the areas of criticizing, discouraging, constricted, tense, and fostering of conformity; and, therefore, she/he decides to select motivation strategies related to the subfactors of "Questions," "Feelings," and "Climate" to emphasize and incorporate in daily motivation plans for the class.

The motivation plan might be:

MOTIVA-TION FACTORS	MOTIVATION STRATEGIES	FUNCTIONAL STRATEGIES
B E G I N N I N G		
(*Attitudes*)	Daily Motivation Plan	Daily Motivation Plan
(*Needs*)	Daily Motivation Plan	Daily Motivation Plan

MOTIVA-TION FACTORS	MOTIVATION STRATEGIES	FUNCTIONAL STRATEGIES
D U R I N G (*Stimulation*) Questions	**1.** Limit the use of knowledge questions, and selectively increase the use of comprehension, application, analysis, synthesis, and evaluation questions.	**1.** Increase the use of synthesis questions, asking students to predict, develop, and create ideas, themes, and meaning from what they are reading during discussion sessions.
	2. Employ M. Sadker and D. Sadker's suggestions for improving the quality of questioning skills that enhance student responsiveness.	**2.** Increase "wait time"—avoid pressuring; avoid frequent evaluative comments; avoid "yes . . . but" reactions; and more often probe the student's answers.
(*Affect*) Feelings	**4.** Whenever a student's feelings seem relevant but are unstated or ambiguous, check your impression of them to open communication and facilitate motivation.	**4.** Check out feelings and actively listen to student responses during discussions.
Climate	**1.** Use Gibb's supportive communication behavior to facilitate a positive climate.	**1.** Avoid communications that imply superiority, control, and dogmatism; increase speech that con-

MOTIVA-TION FACTORS	MOTIVATION STRATEGIES	FUNCTIONAL STRATEGIES
D U R I N G		veys empathy, a problem orientation, equality, and exploration.
	5. Use "climate surveys" to diagnose your classroom atmosphere.	5. In three weeks post-test with the "climate survey" to check on the progress of the classroom atmosphere.
E N D I N G	(Competence) Daily Motivation Plan	Daily Motivation Plan
	(Reinforcement) Daily Motivation Plan	Daily Motivation Plan

Again, the above two examples stress the three guidelines mentioned earlier in this chapter:

1. Planning of motivation strategies along a time frame that maximizes their effectiveness.

2. Use of motivation strategies related to each of the six general motivation factors.

3. Use of particular strategies that relate to teacher personality, learning situation, subject matter, and student characteristics.

With one additional guideline:

4. Continual emphasis of preventive or restorative motivation strategies to inhibit further problem development and to restore higher student motivation.

The additional guideline will be far less effective if not employed in context with the other three. We can often make a mistake when we add strategies but eliminate the other vital parts of the total approach.

As I mentioned in the outset of this book, student motivation seems to be more complex than I'd like it to be. But I respect this and encourage a "leave no stone unturned" approach. This will be difficult and challenging for us as teachers. Yet, I know of no other means that I can easily accept today. Perhaps the following verse says it best:

> If I feel good about learning
> Do I also want to
> And if I do
> Am I stimulated
> And if I am
> Can I enjoy the people with whom I learn
> And if I can
> Do I feel more effective as a result of this learning
> And if I do
> Am I reinforced when I finish it
> And if I am
> I guess I have been motivated.

Some Final Comments

Very little has been written in this book regarding exceptional groups of students such as the gifted, the slow learners, the mentally retarded, etc. There are two reasons for this. The first is basically philosophical in nature while the second is related to my knowledge of students and their particular needs.

Every student, as well as every class, is exceptional. By this, I mean that they are unique. They have their own specific attitudes, their own special needs, their own particular ways of relating and being stimulated, their own individual sense of competence, and their own favorite reinforcers—all of which combine to make the student or group of students a one-of-a-kind experience for us as teachers. Therefore, I resist offering formulas of motivation for the exceptional student when I basically believe the term to be a misnomer. This is not to say that there are not certain kinds of students—the retarded, those in particular age groups such as early elementary and junior high, etc.—that when found in groups do not display behaviors and characteristics that are often similarly patterned. There are. But I do not possess the confident knowledge (if such does exist) to comprehensively and professionally suggest motivation strategies that have a high probability of distinctively improving student motivation for those particular groups in a manner that would not require another book of this size and magnitude. And I do not want to be overly simplistic or rely on clichés.

Thus, I suggest that you incorporate what has been written in this book and fit it to your "exceptional" student or group in a manner that relates to the special talents and individual characteristics of that person or class, based on your knowledge and awareness of these.

Another topic that I have not discussed is the involvement of parents as facilitators of student motivation. I have both respect and apprehension regarding the utilization of parents to increase student motivation. It is a common occurrence in teaching to invite parents to a conference when their child is not motivated for school learning. In positive support of this approach, I can state that (1) parents should be aware of motivation problems related to their children (they have a right to this awareness as consumers of public education); (2) parents can help to facilitate the motivation to learn in their children (they are often a fine resource of methods and insights that can be of immense help to the teacher); and (3) parents can support the motivation strategies of the teacher (they can supplement at home through cooperative planning with the teacher means and ways to enhance the motivation of their children). However, there are some negative possibilities that can result from parental involvement in the effort to facilitate student motivation. Some of the more infamous are as follows:

1. *Parents, disappointed and angry with their children, may threaten and coerce them to learn.* Rather than enhancing motivation, they only continue the student's sense of imprisonment and further rejection of school and related learning experiences. The student may often show a gain in performance but will continue to dislike learning, and this attitude that eventually leads to the rejection of education as a vital lifelong experience will be strengthened.

2. *When a teacher invites parents to help resolve motivation problems, she/he may be seen by the student as directly responsible for any negative consequences that befall the student.* In this manner, the teacher becomes to the student

an informer who has caused the threat and coercion the student is now facing. This may only increase student resentment and hostility toward the teacher and the learning situation. Again, at best, learning may increase, but the student–teacher relationship has a prisoner–warden quality which inhibits any enjoyment or trust.

3. *Teachers may become too dependent on parents for assistance to facilitate student motivation.* Without parental assistance, we may feel hopeless and give up our responsibility for facilitating student motivation. I sometimes hear comments from teachers that are summarized by these two sentences: "The parents don't even care. What can I do?" This is certainly valid and unfortunately not infrequent. However, my position regarding teacher frustration because parents do not support their children's education is that generally it is beyond our means and not benefited by our emotional grief. We are not social workers, and we are usually powerless to change home environments or to rehabilitate parents. What we can do, and are professionally responsible for doing, is to construct the best learning situation possible. This is usually done in the classroom and best served by our personal investment of effort and emotion toward it. We need to be aware of parental influence on our students, but we cannot afford to be intimidated by parents who do not support student learning. If parents will not cooperate, that is a fact we accept—something we must remain aware of, but not be defeated by in our role as educators. Parental cooperation is, in my opinion, a bonus, not a requirement for effective teaching. If we wait for those parents who do not care to begin to care, we are only increasing a motivational vacuum that the classroom need not be. Our efforts, the learning situation, student peer groups, and teaching methods can still have an impact that, although not omnipotent, will be more effective with our faith than without it.

Therefore, when inviting parents to help resolve student motivation problems, a few guidelines may be helpful:

1. *Place the motivational concerns within the total context of the student's personality and learning behavior.* Parents need

190

to see the positive aspects as well as the negative ramifications of the student's behavior. We do not want to alarm them or cause an overreaction to the problem. We need to guard against any approach on their part that might be punitive or too severe in its demands.

2. *Involve the parents and the student in the decision-making process that seeks to resolve the motivational problem.* Ask for their suggestions and reactions. (The conflict resolution method found in Chapter 5 is an excellent model to employ.) Their participation will enhance their motivation to cooperate and follow through on whatever is decided.

3. *If the parents and/or the student is not cooperative, leave the door open for their involvement at a later date.* Sometimes parental or student defensiveness or mistrust does not allow for immediate positive input. However, with time, trust and confidence may be established. Concluding an uncooperative session by indicating some hope for future participation allows the parents or student a means to re-enter without losing face or suffering embarrassment.

The last item I wish to discuss is our own motivation as teachers. How do we continue to facilitate our motivation throughout the days, months, and years of our teaching? The best insight I have is that motivated students help motivate teachers, and motivated teachers help motivate students. The cycle usually begins with us because we bear the responsibility as professional educators. What I want to emphasize is that *every time we facilitate student motivation to learn, we are directly contributing to our own motivation to teach.* Those smiling, enthusiastic faces, those moments of insight and wonder, those student expressions of completion and accomplishment, and those heads held upright and eyes wide that say, "I did it; I learned something," are the force that gives life to our work. Experience them. They occur in any class. By paying attention to them and savoring them, we affirm our existence. We cannot ask for them—we can only see them. Take a look. Then plan, organize, and, above all else, enjoy.

CHAPTER 1

1. Summary of "National School Public Relations Association Task Force on Public Confidence Report" in *The Wisconsin Department of Public Instruction Newsletter* 29:2; February 1977.

CHAPTER 2

1. "We," "us," etc., are used to denote teachers. The author, a teacher, assumes that most of the readers of the book are teachers as well.

2. Rogers, C. R. *Freedom to Learn.* Columbus, Ohio: Charles E. Merrill, 1969. Johnson, D. W. *Reaching Out: Interpersonal Effectiveness and Self-Actualization.* Englewood Cliffs, N.J.: Prentice-Hall, Inc., 1972. Gordon, T. *Teacher Effectiveness Training.* New York: Peter H. Wyden, 1974.

3. In *Schools Without Failure* (New York: Harper & Row, 1969), Glasser recommends this approach as a regular classroom event.

4. For a more elaborate discussion of this method, see Johnson, D. W. *Reaching Out: Interpersonal Effectiveness and Self-Actualization.*

5. Mager, R. F. *Developing Attitude Toward Learning.* Belmont, Calif.: Fearon, 1968. p. 39.

6. R. F. Mager presents an excellent discussion of this strategy in *Developing Attitude Toward Learning.*

7. Each of these conditions will be elaborated upon relative to their specific motivation subfactors that follow in this book.

8. For a detailed discussion of this method, see Ellis, A. *Reason and Emotion in Psychotherapy.* New York: Lyle Stuart, 1962.

9. Scott, J. P. "A Time to Learn." *Psychology Today* 2:67; March 1969.

10. Elkins, D. P., editor. *Glad to Be Me.* Englewood Cliffs, N.J.: Prentice-Hall, 1976. p. 37.

11. Combs, A. W. "Some Basic Concepts in Perceptual Psychology." Paper presented at the American Personnel and Guidance Convention, Minneapolis, April 1965. Rogers, C. R. *Freedom to Learn.* Columbus, Ohio: Charles E. Merrill, 1969.

12. Combs, A. W., *loc. cit.*

13. Seligman, M. *Helplessness.* San Francisco: Freeman, 1975.

14. An excellent review and research of this theory are found in de Charms, R. *Enhancing Motivation: Change in the Classroom.* New York: Irvington, 1976.

15. Canfield, J., and Wells, H. C. *One Hundred Ways to Enhance Self-Concept in the Classroom.* Englewood Cliffs, N.J.: Prentice-Hall, Inc., 1975.

16. For an excellent discussion of these methods, see Dunn, R., and Dunn, K. *Practical Approaches to Individualizing Instruction: Contracts and Other Effective Teaching Strategies.* West Nyack, N.Y.: Parker, 1972.

CHAPTER 3

1. Maslow, A. H. *Toward a Psychology of Being.* Second edition. Princeton, N.J.: Van Nostrand, 1968. Maslow, A. H. *Motivation and Personality.* Second edition. New York: Harper & Row, 1970.

2. Maslow, A. H. *Motivation and Personality.* p. 102.

3. Maslow, A. H. *Toward A Psychology of Being.* pp. 45 46.

4. *Ibid.,* pp. 58–59.

5. *Ibid.,* p. 47.

6. Glasser, W. *The Identity Society.* New York: Harper & Row, 1972.

7. Glasser, W. *Schools Without Failure.* New York: Harper & Row, 1969.

8. A good resource for this approach is Block, J., editor. *Mastery Learning: Theory and Practice.* New York: Holt, Rinehart and Winston, 1971.

9. Colangelo, N.; Foxely, C.; and Dustin, D., editors. *Multicultural Nonsexist Education.* Dubuque, Iowa: Kendall/Hunt, 1979.

10. Schreiber, D., and Kaplin, B., editors. *Guidance and the School Dropout*. Washington, D.C.: National Education Association, 1964.

11. This definition is from Mayesky, M., Neuman, D., and Wlodkowki, R. J. *Creative Activities for Young Children*. Albany, N.Y.: Delmar, 1975.

CHAPTER 4

1. Korman, A. *The Psychology of Motivation*. Englewood Cliffs, N.J.: Prentice-Hall, Inc., 1974.

2. For an excellent discussion of lesson presentation skills, see Cooper, J. M., editor. *Classroom Teaching Skills: A Handbook*. Lexington, Mass.: D. C. Heath, 1977.

3. Kounin, J. S. *Discipline and Group Management in Classrooms*. New York: Holt, Rinehart, and Winston, 1970.

4. Shostak, R. "Lesson Presentation Skills." *Classroom Teaching Skills: A Handbook*. (Edited by J. M. Cooper.) Lexington, Mass.: D. C. Heath, 1977. pp. 121-154.

5. If you have no audiovisual equipment, find a trustworthy observer.

6. For a book with many positive suggestions in this area, see Stanford, G., and Roark, A. E. *Human Interaction in Education*. Boston: Allyn and Bacon, 1974.

7. For a humanistic approach to sports and games, see Orlick, T., and Botterill, C. *Every Kid Can Win*. Chicago: Nelson-Hall, 1974.

8. Sadker, M., and Sadker, D. "Questioning Skills." *Classroom Teaching Skills: A Handbook*. (Edited by J. M. Cooper.) Lexington, Mass.: D. C. Heath, 1977. pp. 155-192.

9. See Bloom, B., editor. *Taxonomy of Education Objectives: Handbook I Cognitive Domain*. New York: David McKay, 1956.

10. For a comprehensive treatment of this strategy, see Hunkins, F. P. *Questioning Strategies and Techniques*. Boston: Allyn and Bacon, 1972.

11. Adapted from Sadker, M., and Sadker, D. "Questioning Skills" in Cooper, J. M., editor. *Classroom Teaching Skills: A Handbook*.

12. *Ibid*.

13. Bigge, M. *Learning Theories for Teachers*. New York: Harper & Row, 1976.

CHAPTER 5

1. Castillo, G. *Left-Handed Teaching*. New York: Praeger Publishers, 1974.

2. Weinstein, G., and Fantini, M. *Toward Humanistic Education: A Curriculum of Affect*. New York: Praeger Publishers, 1970.

3. *Ibid.*

4. Ideas for this exercise are adapted from Wackman, D., Miller, S., and Nunnally, E. *Student Workbook: Increasing Awareness and Communication Skills*. Minneapolis: International Communication Programs, Inc., 300 Clifton Avenue, 1976.

5. Although I have attempted to list those strategies that I believe are critical to awareness and communication of feelings relevant to motivation, I realize that my suggestions are limited in scope and comprehensiveness. Entire books have been written on these strategies. The top six on my list, in alphabetical order, are:

    a. Gazda, G. *Human Relations Development*. Boston: Allyn and Bacon, Inc., 1973.

    b. Gordon, T. *Teacher Effectiveness Training*. New York: Peter H. Wyden, Inc., 1972.

    c. Johnson, D. W. *Reaching Out: Interpersonal Effectiveness and Self-Actualization*. Englewood Cliffs, N.J.: Prentice-Hall, Inc., 1972.

    d. Luft, J. *Group Process: An Introduction to Group Dynamics*. Second edition. Palo Alto, Calif.: National Press Books, 1970.

    e. Lyon, H. *Learning to Feel—Feeling to Learn*. Columbus, Ohio: Charles E. Merrill Publishing Co., 1971.

    f. Schmuck, R., and Schmuck, P. *Group Processes in the Classroom*. Dubuque, Iowa: William C. Brown Co., 1971.

6. Gordon calls this *active listening* and presents an excellent discussion of it in *Teacher Effectiveness Training*.

7. Often called *I-messages* or *assertiveness* by other theorists.

8. See Brown, G. I. *Human Teaching for Human Learning*. New York: Viking Press, 1971. Brown, G. I., editor. *The Live Classroom*. New York: Viking Press, 1975.

9. Castillo, *op. cit.*

10. Weinstein, G., and Fantini, M., *op. cit.*

11. *Ibid.*

12. Raths, L., Harmin, M., and Simon, S. *Values and Teaching.* Columbus, Ohio: Charles E. Merrill, 1967.

13. Kirschenbaum, H., Harmin, M., Howe, L., and Simon, S. "In Defense of Values Clarification." *Phi Delta Kappan,* June 1977.

14. For a current list of the many books, materials, and kits available in this area, write to the National Humanistic Education Center, Springfield Road, Upper Jay, New York 12987.

15. Schmuck, R., and Schmuck, P. *A Humanistic Psychology of Education.* Palo Alto, Calif.: National Press Books, 1974.

16. *Ibid.,* p. 189.

17. Gibb, J. "Defensive Communication." *The Journal of Communication* 11: 141–48; September 1961.

18. For an excellent treatment of this strategy, see Johnson, D. W., and Johnson, R. T. *Learning Together and Alone.* Englewood Cliffs, N.J.: Prentice-Hall, Inc., 1975.

19. For an excellent resource for group process skills, see Johnson, D. W., and Johnson, F. P. *Joining Together: Group Theory and Group Skills.* Englewood Cliffs, N.J.: Prentice-Hall, Inc., 1975.

20. *Ibid.,* pp. 60–61.

21. Gordon, T., *op. cit.*

22. Adapted from Johnson, D. W., and Johnson, F. P., *op. cit.*

CHAPTER 6

1. White, R. W. "Motivation Reconsidered: The Concept of Competence." *Psychological Review* 66: 297–333; 1959.

2. *Ibid.*

3. White, R. W. "Competence as a Basic Concept in the Growth of Personality." Paper prepared for the Social Science Research Council's Conference on The Socialization and Evaluation of Competence, San Juan, Puerto Rico, 1965.

4. *Ibid.*

5. Nardine, F. "The Development of Competence." *Psychology and Educational Practice.* (Edited by G. Lesser.) Glenview, Ill.: Scott, Foresman and Co., 1971.

6. *Ibid.,* pp. 337.

7. Alschuler, A. S. *Developing Achievement Motivation in Adolescents.* Englewood Cliffs, N.J.: Educational Technology Publications, 1973.

8. de Charms, R., *op. cit.*

9. de Charms, R. *Personal Causation.* New York: Academic Press, 1968. p. 269.

10. de Charms, R. *Enhancing Motivation: Change in the Classroom.* p. 74.

11. *Ibid.*

12. J. S. Coleman's major national research, as described in *Equality of Education Opportunity* (Washington, D.C.: Government Printing Office, 1966), found student self-concept and the degree to which students believed they could control their own destiny as having more of an effect on learning than teacher training, physical facilities, or curricula combined.

13. The following books provide excellent and detailed suggestions for feedback as well as individualization related to learning:
    a. Block, J., editor. *Mastery Learning: Theory and Practice.* New York: Holt, Rinehart & Winston, 1971.
    b. Bloom, B., Hastings, T., and Madaus, G., editors. *Handbook on Formative and Summative Evaluation of Student Learning.* New York: McGraw-Hill, 1971.
    c. Blackburn, J., and Powell, W. *One at a Time, All at Once.* Santa Monica, Calif.: Goodyear Publishing Co., Inc., 1976.

14. Bloom, B. "Learning for Mastery." *Evaluation Comment.* Los Angeles: Center for the Study of Evaluation of Instructional Programs, 1968.

15. *Ibid.,* p. 1.

16. This definition is from Sharp, B. *Learning the Rhythm of Risk.* Rosemont, Ill.: Combined Motivation Education Systems, 1971.

17. Most of these are thoroughly discussed in *Learning Together and Alone* by Johnson and Johnson. Their comprehensive treatment of cooperation, competition, and individualization is an excellent teacher resource.

18. Olgilvie, B., and Tutko, T. "Sport: If You Want to Build Character, Try Something Else." *Psychology Today* 5: 60–63; 1971.

CHAPTER 7

1. The definitions and conceptual framework of this section are based on the review of reinforcement theory and related research found in Glaser, R., and Cooley, W. "Instrumentation for Teaching and Instructional Management." *Second Handbook of Research on Teaching.* (Edited by R. Travers.) Chicago: Rand McNally, 1973. pp. 832–57.

2. Entire books have been written that employ a total reinforcement approach to teaching and learning. These are well worth the attention of the teacher for the practical and valuable insights and suggestions they offer. Although I do not agree with some of their basic assumptions and am critical of their one-sided approach to motivation, I continue to maintain that we as professional educators cannot afford to deny or to ignore what we may not comprehend. Therefore, we must first understand the substance of reinforcement theory before we accept, select, or reject any or all of its theoretical and functional ideas for learning. Some of the most helpful texts in this area are:

   a. Becker, W., Engelmann, S., and Thomas, D. *Teaching: A Course in Applied Psychology.* Chicago: Science Research Associates, 1971.

   b. Homme, L., and Tosti, D. *Behavior Technology: Motivation and Contingency Management.* San Rafael, Calif.: Individual Learning Systems, 1971.

   c. Krumboltz, J., and Krumboltz, H. *Changing Children's Behavior.* Englewood Cliffs, N.J.: Prentice-Hall, Inc., 1972.

   d. Skinner, B. F. *The Technology of Teaching.* New York: Appleton-Century-Crofts, 1968.

   e. Vargas, J. *Behavioral Psychology For Teachers.* New York: Harper & Row, 1977.

3. Calder, B. J., and Staw, B. M. "Self Perception of Intrinsic and Extrinsic Motivation," *Journal of Personality and Social Psychology* 31: 599–605; 1975.

4. Staw, B. M. *Intrinsic and Extrinsic Motivation.* University Programs Modular Studies. Morristown, N.J.: General Learning Press, 1976.

5. Bijou, S. W. "What Psychology Has to Offer Education—Now." *Journal of Applied Behavior Analysis* 3:65–71; Spring 1970.

6. Although the concept of a reinforcer can theoretically be divided into positive and negative reinforcers, I respect Skinner's warning regarding the misuse of and aversive by-products of negative reinforcement and choose to omit it from the strategy.

7. Vargas, J. S. *Behavioral Psychology for Teachers*. New York: Harper & Row, 1977.

8. For a description of these alternatives, as well as others, in detail, see Kirschenbaum, H., Simon, S., and Napier, R. *WAD-JA-GET: The Grading Game in American Education*. New York: Hart, 1971. Bellanca, J. A. *Grading*. Washington, D.C.: National Education Association, 1977.

9. For a comprehensive review of this strategy, see Johnson, D. W., and Johnson, R. T. *Learning Together and Alone*.

CHAPTER 8

1. These numbers are correlated to the strategies and factors found in Figure 4.

Bibliography

Alschuler, A. S. *Developing Achievement Motivation in Adolescents.* Engle-wood Cliffs, N.J.: Educational Technology Publications, 1973.

Ball, S., editor. *Motivation in Education.* New York: Academic Press, 1977.

Becker, W., Engelmann, S., and Thomas, D. *Teaching: A Course in Applied Psychology.* Chicago: Science Research Associates, 1971.

Bellanca, J. A. *Grading.* Washington, D.C.: National Education Association, 1977.

Biehler, R. F. *Psychology Applied to Teaching.* Second edition. Boston: Houghton Mifflin, 1974.

Bigge, M. *Learning Theories for Teachers.* New York: Harper & Row, 1976.

Bijou, S. W. "What Psychology Has to Offer Education—Now." *Journal of Applied Behavior Analysis* 3:65–71; Spring 1970.

Blackburn, J., and Powell, W. *One at a Time, All at Once.* Santa Monica, Calif.: Goodyear, 1976.

Block, J., editor. *Mastery Learning: Theory and Practice.* New York: Holt, Rinehart and Winston, 1971.

Bloom, B. "Learning for Mastery." *Evaluation Comment.* Los Angeles: Center for the Study of Evaluation of Instructional Programs, 1968.

————, editor. *Taxonomy of Educational Objectives, Handbook I Cognitive Domain.* New York: David McKay, 1956.

————, Hastings, T., and Madaus, G., editors. *Handbook on Formative and Summative Evaluation of Student Learning.* New York: McGraw-Hill, 1971.

————. *Human Characteristics and School Learning.* New York: McGraw-Hill, 1976.

Brown, G. I. *Human Teaching for Human Learning.* New York: Viking Press, 1971.

————, editor. *The Live Classroom.* New York: Viking Press, 1975.

Calder, B. J. and Staw, B. M. "Self-Perception of Intrinsic and Extrinsic Motivation." *Journal of Personality and Social Psychology* 31: 599–605; 1975.

Campbell, S. *Expanding Your Teaching Potential.* Amherst, Mass.: Mandala Press, 1977.

Canfield, J. and Wells, H. C. *One Hundred Ways to Enhance Self-Concept in the Classroom.* Englewood Cliffs, N.J.: Prentice-Hall, 1975.

Castillo, G. *Left-Handed Teaching.* New York: Praeger Publishers, 1974.

Coleman, J. S., and others. *Equality of Educational Opportunity.* Washington, D.C.: Government Printing Office, 1966.

Combs, A. W. "Some Basic Concepts in Perceptual Psychology." Paper read at American Personnel and Guidance Convention, Minneapolis, April 1965.

Cooper, J., editor. *Classroom Teaching Skills: A Handbook.* Lexington, Mass.: D. C. Heath, 1977.

de Charms, R. *Enhancing Motivation: Change in the Classroom.* New York: Irvington, 1976.

————. *Personal Causation.* New York: Academic Press, 1968.

Dinkmeyer, D. C., and McKay, G. *Raising a Responsible Child.* New York: Simon and Schuster, 1973.

Dreikurs, R., Grunwald, B. B., and Pepper, F. C. *Maintaining Sanity in the Classroom.* New York: Harper & Row, 1971.

Dunn, R., and Dunn, K. *Practical Approaches to Individualizing Instruction: Contracts and Other Effective Teaching Strategies.* West Nyack, N.Y.: Parker, 1972.

Elkins, D. P., editor. *Glad to Be Me.* Englewood Cliffs, N.J.: Prentice-Hall, 1976.

Ellis, A. *Reason and Emotion in Psychotherapy.* New York: Lyle Stuart, 1962.

Flavell, J. H. *The Developmental Psychology of Jean Piaget*. New York: Van Nostrand, 1963.

Gazda, G. *Human Relations Development*. Boston: Allyn and Bacon, 1973.

Gibb, J. "Defensive Communication." *The Journal of Communication* 11: 141–148; September 1961.

Glaser, R., and Cooley, W. "Instrumentation for Teaching and Instructional Management." *Second Handbook of Research on Teaching.* (Edited by R. Travers.) Chicago: Rand McNally, 1973. pp. 832–857.

Glasser, W. *Schools Without Failure*. New York: Harper & Row, 1969.

————. *The Identity Society*. New York: Harper & Row, 1972.

Gordon, T. *Teacher Effectiveness Training*. New York: Peter H. Wyden, 1974.

Herrnstein, R. J. "The Evolution of Behaviorism." *American Psychologist* 32: 593–603; 1977.

Homme, L., and Tosti, D. *Behavior Technology: Motivation and Contingency Management*. San Rafael, Calif.: Individual Learning Systems, 1971.

Hunkins, F. P. *Questioning Strategies and Techniques*. Boston: Allyn and Bacon, 1972.

Hunt, J. McV. *Intelligence and Experience*. New York: Ronald Press, 1961.

Johnson, D. W. *Reaching Out: Interpersonal Effectiveness and Self-Actualization*. Englewood Cliffs, N.J.: Prentice-Hall, 1972.

————, and Johnson, F. P. *Joining Together: Group Theory and Group Skills*. Englewood Cliffs, N.J.: Prentice-Hall, 1975.

————, and Johnson, R. T. *Learning Together and Alone*. Englewood Cliffs, N.J.: Prentice-Hall, 1975.

Kanfer, F. H., and Goldstein, A. P., editors. *Helping People Change: A Textbook of Methods*. New York: Pergamon, 1975.

Kirschenbaum, H., Harmin, M., Howe, L., and Simon, S. "In Defense of Values Clarification." *Phi Delta Kappan*, June 1977.

Kirschenbaum, H., Simon, S., and Napier, R. *WAD-JA-GET: The Grading Game in American Education*. New York: Hart, 1971.

Korman, A. *The Psychology of Motivation.* Englewood Cliffs, N.J.: Prentice-Hall, 1974.

Kounin, J. S. *Discipline and Group Management in Classrooms.* New York: Holt, Rinehart and Winston, 1970.

Krumboltz, J. D., and Krumboltz, H. B. *Changing Children's Behavior.* Englewood Cliffs, N.J.: Prentice-Hall, 1972.

Lefcourt, H. M. *Locus of Control.* New York: Wiley, 1976.

Lesser, G., editor. *Psychology and Educational Practice.* Glenview, Ill.: Scott, Foresman, 1971.

Luft, J. *Group Process: An Introduction to Group Dynamics.* Second edition. Palo Alto, Calif.: National Press Books, 1970.

Lyon, H. *Learning to Feel—Feeling to Learn.* Columbus, Ohio: Charles E. Merrill, 1971.

Mager, R. F. *Developing Attitude Toward Learning.* Belmont, Calif.: Fearon, 1968.

Maslow, A. H. *Motivation and Personality.* Second edition. New York: Harper & Row, 1970.

————. *Toward a Psychology of Being.* Second edition. Princeton, N.J.: Van Nostrand, 1968.

Mayesky, M., Neuman, D., and Wlodkowski, R. J. *Creative Activities for Young Children.* Albany, N.Y.: Delmar, 1975.

Miller, S., Nunnally, E. W., and Wackman, D. B. *Alive and Aware: Improving Communication in Relationships.* Minneapolis: Interpersonal Communications Programs, 1975.

Noar, G. *The Teacher and Integration.* Washington, D.C.: National Education Association, 1974.

Olgilvie, B., and Tutko, T. "Sport: If You Want to Build Character, Try Something Else." *Psychology Today* 5: 60–63; 1971.

Orlick, T., and Botterill, C. *Every Kid Can Win.* Chicago: Nelson–Hall, 1974.

Raths, L., Harmin, M., and Simon, S. *Values and Teaching.* Columbus, Ohio: Charles E. Merrill, 1967.

Rogers, C. R. *Freedom to Learn*. Columbus, Ohio: Charles E. Merrill, 1969.

Schmuck, R., and Schmuck, P. *A Humanistic Psychology of Education*. Palo Alto, Calif.: National Press Books, 1974.

_____. *Group Processes in the Classroom*. Dubuque, Iowa: William C. Brown, 1971.

Schreiber, D., and Kaplin, B., editors. *Guidance and the School Dropout*. Washington, D.C.: National Education Association, 1964.

Scott, J. P. "A Time to Learn." *Psychology Today* 2:67; March 1969.

Seligman, M. *Helplessness*. San Francisco: Freeman, 1975.

Sharp, B. *Learning the Rhythm of Risk*. Rosemont, Ill.: Combined Motivation Education Systems, 1971.

Skinner, B. F. *The Technology of Teaching*. New York: Appleton-Century-Crofts, 1968.

Stanford, G., and Roark, A. E. *Human Interaction in Education*. Boston: Allyn and Bacon, 1974.

Staw, B. M. *Intrinsic and Extrinsic Motivation*. University Program Modular Studies. Morristown, N.J.: General Learning Press, 1976.

Vargas, J. *Behavioral Psychology for Teachers*. New York: Harper & Row, 1977.

Wackman, D., Miller, S., and Nunnally, E. *Student Workbook: Increasing Awareness and Communication Skills*. Minneapolis: Interpersonal Communication Programs, Inc., 1976.

Weinstein, G., and Fantini, M. *Toward Humanistic Education: A Curriculum of Affect*. New York: Praeger Publishers, 1970.

White, R. W. "Competence as a Basic Concept in the Growth of Personality." Paper prepared for the Social Science Research Council's Conference on the Socialization and Evaluation of Competence, San Juan, Puerto Rico, 1965.

_____. "Motivation Reconsidered: The Concept of Competence." *Psychological Review* 66: 297–333; 1959.

Wlodkowski, R. J. "A Practical Model for Motivation." *Impact* ERIC, 3: 35–39; 1974.

_____. "Counseling and Motivation in Synergistic Education." *Counseling and Values* 18: 18–21; 1973.

————. *Motivation*. Washington, D.C.: National Education Association, 1977.

————. "The Effect of Dissonance and Arousal on Assignment Performance as They Relate to Student Expectancy and Teacher Support Characteristics." *The Journal of Educational Research* 67: 23–28; 1973.

Index